RECORDER
of DEEDS

Praise for Recorder of Deeds

"A powerful story about resilience and the importance of emotional connections when called upon to brave overwhelming stress." — George Faller, FDNY Lieutenant (ret.), Licensed Marital and Family Therapist, Author of *Sacred Stress*

"My colleague at the *Milwaukee Journal Sentinel*, Catherine Fitzpatrick, is a gifted writer, reporter, and author with a descriptive writing style, and the ability to convey emotions, hers and others. I deeply appreciated our shared story-telling during the week of 9/11 in New York. We powered through the pain to bring out a world-changing story even as we dealt with the emotional trauma of those tragic days." — Richard Wood, Staff Photographer, *Milwaukee Journal Sentinel*, retired

"For those who never penned their life's story because it would be painfully dull, *Recorder of Deeds* will confirm you made the right decision. This memoir by a lover of words presents a family far more interesting than fictional characters!" — Anita B. Lamont, Former Features Editor, *St. Louis Globe-Democrat*, Retired Senior Director Communications, Charter Communications

"My sister is a storyteller. This story of hers, of ours, is heartwarming, heart-rending, honest, and true down to the last detail. I know. I was there for much of it." — Kenneth James Underhill, Catherine Underhill Fitzpatrick's brother

"What is it like to stand near Ground Zero on 9/11, watching the Twin Towers dissolve into dust and debris even as you and your siblings survive the weight of multiple deaths, mental illness, drug addiction, and more? In *Recorder of Deeds*, an award-winning journalist answers that question in gut-wrenching yet ultimately uplifting detail. At a time when our world has 'razor-sharp edges,' Fitzpatrick shows us that 'the heart is a wondrous thing.'" — Karla Linn Merrifield, Poet and Author, *Psyche's Scroll*, *Athabaskan Fractal: Poems of the Far North*

"Good times, bad times and all those times in between are the threads that weave the tapestry of our lives. In her new memoir, Catherine unravels the threads of her life to bravely share her experiences, some of them devastating, but many simply glorious." — Karen K. Marshall, Former editor, *St. Louis Globe-Democrat*, Retired Director, Industry Relations, The Monsanto Company

"*Recorder of Deeds* presents a verbal picture that forces the reader to care for Catherine and her family. The details of major events and minor are told with an amazing attention to detail that makes you believe you are there, sometimes right in the hospital room with her. Her recounting of experiences of covering the 9/11 attack on the World Trade Center and the positives and negatives of family life produce a fascinating and enjoyable read." — Lowell W. Gerson, Professor Emeritus of Family and Community Medicine, Northeast Ohio Medical University

"In this era of ubiquitous memoirs, here is one you should read. Catherine Underhill Fitzpatrick took a ten-year slice of her life and, being the clear-eyed journalist she is, chronicled professional awards and an embarrassing fall from grace, family heartache and discord, and her on-the-scene experiences with the worst attack on American soil since Pearl Harbor. Eminently readable, *Recorder of Deeds* is a full-throttle dash through a decade that leaves the reader a bit dizzy and wondering how the writer maintained her sanity." — Damien Jaques, Reporter and arts critic, retired, *Milwaukee Journal Sentinel*

"In *Recorder of Deeds*, Catherine takes us along on her ten-year journey, a story that reveals the resilience of the human spirit and the universal truth that family is the tie that binds. With a fine eye for detail and lushly written observations, Fitzpatrick grabs our attention in the opening sentences and leaves us sputtering, 'Tell me more.'" — Carol S. Cole, Former Features Editor, *St. Louis Globe Democrat*

"Reading *Recorder of Deeds* is akin to taking a long walk through the highs and lows, the triumphs and losses that make up a life well lived. Here is a woman who faces a mirror of memories without a blink. To open her life to others, many of whom she will never meet, is an act of courage. Any and all who join her story will see reflections of their own lives. It is a comfort to know that none of us is alone during the struggles and joys of living." — Miles Goodwin, Contributing essayist, *This I Believe: The Personal Philosophies of Remarkable Men and Women*

"*Recorder of Deeds* is a compelling page turner. Catherine is expert at capturing the sights, sounds and imagery of everything she describes, and the storytelling of her presence at the events of 9/11 is breathtaking. This memoir is clear evidence of Catherine's rich and full life." — Debra Valentina, Author of *Beyond Chaos: Journey to Freedom and Joy*

"*Recorder of Deeds* lovingly and richly chronicles the history of a family and, beyond that, a slice of America. Catherine's well-crafted prose makes this memoir a compelling read." — Kathleen Arenz, Former Columnist, *Milwaukee Journal Sentinel*, Past President, Woman's Club of Wisconsin

Also by Catherine Underhill Fiztpatrick

A Matter of Happenstance
Eternal Day
Going on Nine
Voyage: A Memoir of Love, War, and Ever After

RECORDER of DEEDS

Terrorism and Trauma:
A Journalist's Life-Changing Choice on 9/11

Catherine Underhill Fitzpatrick

Bink Books
Bedazzled Ink Publishing Company • Fairfield, California

paperback 978-1-949290-76-9

Cover Design
by

Bink Books
a division of
Bedazzled Ink Publishing, LLC
Fairfield, California
http://www.bedazzledink.com

For my grandchildren

Lillian Leslie Gould
Nolan John Leitenberger
Maeve June Leitenberger

In you, the story lives on

Between 80 and 100% of journalists have been exposed to a work-related traumatic event . . . A significant minority are at risk for long-term psychological problems, including PTSD.[1] — "Covering Trauma: Impact on Journalists"

I dare venture to promise, the judicious reader shall find nothing neglected here . . .[2] — Jonathan Swift

Author's Note

Except where so stated, everything that happens in this memoir happened in real life, every word wrung from memory or extracted from public records and written discourse.

To protect the rights and sentiments of those who did not or could not agree to participate, I paraphrased or summarized their words.

Due to the sensitive nature of issues on these pages, I altered the identity of some individuals and locations.

Catherine Underhill Fitzpatrick

Chapters

Preface

I COME FROM a family of storytellers. In the evenings, my father would stand at the head of the supper table and calculate with practiced eye the meatloaf or chuck roast set before him so that, if dissected with surgical precision, it would go the distance. During the hush that followed, he held six hungry children rapt with stories we knew by heart and asked for by name.[3]

The Dog Who Came to Aunt Lil's Funeral
The Monkey-Wrench Steering Wheel
The Secret Gasoline Signal

This story is mine, a stone I held fast for twenty years. Now, at last, it will join the body of articles, essays, photographs, videos, and personal reminiscences that will inform future generations about the risks to those who brought forth the news on a dark day in American history.

In committing to paper what September 11, 2001 was like for me, I am mindful that during a day of monumental events my role was minute. And yet I am a writer by training, trade, and sheer love of the craft, one who witnessed an epic massacre as it unfolded, rushed toward the field of battle and watched victims fall, stood in the path of certain death and somehow survived, and put into words what I saw, heard, and felt *as it was happening*. It is a story worth telling.

For much of my adult life, I have been a recorder of deeds. Many were close to home. Some were well beyond. One rewrote the destiny of nations. To this day, I carry within me shards of that long-ago trauma.

As for the task at hand, I am able, a former journalist who was indulged and celebrated, then excoriated, and finally erased from the true history of reportage for which I risked my life.

In laying open ten years of my experiences and relationships, I hope to provide context to a period that in ways large and small was defined by trauma and its lasting effects. Buffeted by forces within my control and beyond my wildest imagining, I navigated by dead reckoning, and in so doing I charted a course that spanned the continuum of human emotion, frayed the tensile bonds of blood, and mapped the frontiers of professional and personal obligation.

A decade. A lifetime. An eye-blink. Time enough for terrorism and heroism, for despair beyond comfort and hope beyond reason. Time enough for medicine to fail and humor to heal, for trust to waver and faith to founder and each to return stronger than ever. Time enough to mourn long lives in the transcendent moment they forsake the breathing world, and to herald new lives in the triumphant moment they glide into it, glistening with incipience.

Let the record stand. Let it be passed from mother to son, father to daughter. Let it color every late-night recitation of memories that animate the history of an American journalist. Let it imbue every accounting of my actions and temper every assessment of my character.

This is my story. I tell it now as I lived it then.

Chapter 1
Quality Time
1980s and 1990s

Just me and the prez

THE EDITOR SUMMONS me to her office. We sit kneecap-to-kneecap at a tiny conference table. Beyond the glass partition, the newsroom is watching.

The editor smiles. She never smiles.

This can't be good.

Dwindling circulation and advertising are forcing a sea-change in the competitive nature of newsgathering. Newspapers across the country are cutting staff, reducing page counts, and taking more drastic measures. For years now, I have been a part-time feature writer at the *Milwaukee Sentinel*. But in the spring of 1995, the angst-soaked merger of the *Milwaukee Sentinel* and *Milwaukee Journal* is underway. According to rumors, by the time the dust settles, hundreds of employees will be gone.

This is it. I'm toast.

"What do you want to do at the new *Journal Sentinel?*" the editor asks.

I perk up.

"Write features." *Um, shouldn't that be obvious?*

"How about the fashion beat?" she says.

It isn't a question. Everybody knows the fashion writers for both papers are already out the door.

I am stricken. In the pecking order of the newsroom, a feature writer is somewhere in the middle. A fashion writer is lower than dirt.

"It'll be fun," she says. "You'll get to cover New York Fashion Week."

Wait. No! I don't want to write fashion stories. Nobody reads fashion stories; they just look at the pictures.

During a career as a metro daily feature writer, I have loved the variety of the job. On one assignment, I spent quality time alone in a room with the brother-in-law of the queen of England, Antony Armstrong-Jones, Earl of Snowdon. He was on a world tour to promote a book of his photography. When I asked him about his marriage to Princess Margaret, which was crumbling at the time, the door to the interview room opened as if by magic and I was ushered out. On another occasion, I was alone in a room with the suave heir to a Mafia dynasty. His office was in a beautiful old building that had been declared a historic landmark. Weak December sunlight angled through Venetian blinds, obscuring him in backlighting. He lingered overlong helping me out of my coat and asked if I might like to attend a holiday party he was hosting. Indeed, I would not.

In the name of first-person journalism, I have eaten a sheet of edible paper, endured a mud massage and a fire hose barrage, attended the auction of a Van Gogh discovered in an attic. At the auction of a failed farm, I stood on the far side of a kitchen garden and observed the farmer's wife grimace as she watched everything removable on third-generation soil go for a pittance.

In the summer of 1989, I climbed a ladder in a steady drizzle, wrapped my arm around a roof truss, and chatted with Jimmy Carter.

How, when, where, and why I clung to a rainswept roof alongside a former United States president is a story published long ago. I wrote it, editors reviewed it, copyeditors affixed a headline to it, and rushed it down to the pressroom. Thrumming machines inked my words onto sheaves of dried pine mash and recycled fiber—newsprint. Gigantic presses extruded a ribbon of neatly folded copies of the June 16, 1989, *Milwaukee Sentinel*. In cavernous bays, union men bundled the papers, bound them with twine, and tossed them into trucks headed for the hinterlands. Before dawn, delivery boys flung them onto stoops from Sturtevant to Superior.

The article subscribers read over coffee and slices of Racine Danish Kringle contained only part of the story. Here's the rest:

It was somewhere between utterly cold and impossibly cold, what television meteorologists in Wisconsin called *chilly*. Barely fifty degrees of Fahrenheit with intermittent drizzle, fog in the lowlands, gusty wind. I had a mid-morning appointment with Jimmy Carter. The weather? Pfft. Wasn't on my radar.

The former president and first lady were lending their marquee names— and more—to a Habitat for Humanity construction project on the gritty northern fringe of Milwaukee. In a single week, volunteers would build a row of houses from the ground up. When finished, the houses would be turned over to low-income families who were helping with the work. But for the first three days, blue-black clouds had lumbered across southeast Wisconsin and needled the site with drenching rain. The day of my interview was only slightly drier. Work was behind schedule.

That morning, I dressed with care—summer skirt, linen blouse, hose and heels. I'd be sitting down with a former United States president. Just me and the Prez, shooting the breeze. On the way to the site, I envisioned the scene. The clouds would part. Sunbeams would gild the construction site in buttery hues. A Crayola rainbow would arc over the almost-finished houses.

That's the way it should have been. But since the dawn of time, the chasm between what should be and what is has been a chasm.

By the time I arrived at the site, the rain has slowed to a steady drizzle, a good omen. A Habitat staffer glanced at my press card and waved me to a large white tent. I slalomed across a dun brown tract littered with detritus half sunk in mud. Looking up, I saw the carpenters had managed to complete the wood frames of three houses, including the roof trusses.

A security guy at the entrance to the tent glared at me.

"Ma'am," he said, "they're way behind. The president's trying to get a roof finished before it starts to pour again. He's not coming down for any newspaper interview."

"Oh, I won't keep him very . . ."

"See that ladder over there? You want your interview, you're gonna have to climb."

I squinted into the mist. Twenty feet above the ground, Jimmy Carter was canted at a sharp angle, gripping a ridgepole and hammering plywood to a truss. He was soaked to the skin.

I cut the security guy a look and then assessed the course from here to there. Shoe-sucking mud. Ankle-deep puddles. A sprinkling of bent nails, a jagged piece of brick. Splintered boards, empty soda cans, and broken glass. I made it to the ladder without requiring field surgery and planted an Anne Klein pump on the bottom rung.

The light mist had stopped. It had begun to rain.

My ascent was a tap dance choreographed to thunder. Legs spattered to the knee. Hair clinging to my head in tangled skeins. Skirt billowing with every gust of wind. Having given over my dignity to the weather, I gripped the side rails and levered myself skyward. The word here is *inelegant.* When my face cleared the ceiling joists, I smiled and introduced myself. Mr. Carter's eyes flapped open wide, wider than usual. He was not expecting company on his roof. I went directly to the questions I'd jotted in a fresh reporter's notebook and took down his brief answers. For the next few minutes, we each leaned into our work, ignoring the rain. Not once did the man stop pounding nails into the roof's underlayment.

Back in the newsroom, I daubed at my clothing with paper towels and shucked my nylons into a waste can. At my desk, I discovered that the notebook pages were damp and wrinkled, almost translucent. Worse, they were bare! I had stood on a ladder in a downpour and grilled a former American president about how it felt to be doing business as a rainy-day carpenter, and I had recorded his comments verbatim with a felt-tip pen.

It was not my finest hour, reporter-wise.

Chapter 2
Serious Stories
Late 1990s

The power of that nod

IN A GLASSY office on full view of a newsroom in the throes of a merger, the editor drums her manicured nails on the table, waiting for my answer about the fashion writer job. I square my shoulders and make a bold request.

"Occasionally, I'd like to do serious stories that aren't about high heels and hemlines."

A long beat passes. Ever so slowly, she nods.

Amazing, the power of that nod. In the coming years, it will take me to a seminary garden in Minnesota for a story about the Catholic Church sex abuse scandal. It will take me to a God-forsaken cotton gin town in the Yazoo Delta for a coming-of-age story about a Milwaukee teen on a mission trip.

That nod will bring me to the end of a dirt road in Northern Wisconsin for a personal account of a fashion writer trying to survive a women's survival training camp. There, for the first and only time in my life, I discharged a firearm. To be precise, it was a double-barrel shotgun. The instructor had warned me to keep the butt of the gun against my shoulder, but in the euphoria of the moment, with a clay disc sailing through the air, I forgot. The recoil knocked me clean off my feet.

Years later, my expanded job took me to a place no living soul wants to go. Let me explain:

One day in the winter of 2001, the Features editor strolled up to my desk with a killer of an assignment. "Hey Fitzie," she said, "there's a minister I want you to meet. She preaches to Death Row inmates. How would you like to go with her?"

"To Death Row?"

"In Texas."

Would I like to go? Hell yes.

After securing credentials from the Texas Department of Corrections, I flew with a staff photographer to Dallas and connected with the minister. The following morning, we drove from the small town of Gatesville out into an eternity of dull brown flats studded with brushy cholla cactus. Far ahead, an enormous penitentiary complex eventually came into view, low and forbidding buildings surrounded by concertina wire.

After passing electrified gates, towers with optics and munitions, and reinforced checkpoints, we eased up to the visitor's entrance. Female guards searched us with practiced, probing hands and took everything I had brought with me except a small pencil and sheets of paper. The place was giving me the creeps already.

The Death Row cellblock was sequestered deep within the vast compound, a windowless cube of enclosures monitored day and night.

The minister was a cheery, sweet-faced woman in her early fifties. She began by extending greetings and blessings to the handful of inmates who lived on The Row. Then she lowered herself to sit cross-legged on the concrete floor in front of the nearest cell. I dropped down beside her and wrote what she said to a felon convicted of a heinous crime. After a moment or two, I glanced through the bars and quickly looked away, for I was shocked at how young the inmate was, how pretty she was. She had put on makeup and done her hair for our visit, achieving an uncanny likeness to a Texas high school cheerleader.

On the drive back to Gatesville, I asked the minister what the young woman had done to deserve such a harsh sentence.

"Enough," the minister said, speaking softly. "Enough."

Later, I learned the reason: the pretty young prisoner had been convicted of fatally stabbing her five-year-old son with a butcher knife.

Soon after the merger in 1995, I discovered I could create a new kind of fashion beat and make it my own. Soon, I was writing quirky stories about underwear, about the internal engineering of a ballet dancer costume, about Harry Potter clothes for kids, and about Evita Peron getups for women who want to look like Evita Peron.

One fine day back then, I found myself at the fifty-yard line of Lambeau Field, standing in the considerable shadow of a Green Bay Packer.

In Wisconsin, any story about the Packers is big news. So I suggested a story about the protective gear Packers team members wear on game day. The layout would be a full newspaper page, and the graphics designers want me to list everything. Well, nearly everything. A staff photographer and I met one of the team's PR guys outside the stadium. He gave us a quick tour of the locker rooms and then we walked out onto the field of play. It was a weekday afternoon. No game. No practice. Every seat in the stadium was empty.

Fullback William Terrelle Henderson and his agent were waiting for us at mid-field. Henderson was suited up in a team helmet, jersey, shoulder pads, gold pants, the works.

I tossed him a smile. "Nice to meet you."

"Mm-hmm." He looked down at me, his expression impassive.

Best get started.

"Could you take off your clothes, please? Slowly?"

He could and he did. Soon, the man was down to his skivvies.

As I said, some assignments are more fun than others. Most of my time after the merger was devoted to traditional fashion coverage in Milwaukee. But once in a while a routine story turned into a novel experience. The teacup story, for example.

I wrote a piece about Jackie Kennedy's iconic style and almost immediately after it published I received a scathing letter from designer Oleg Cassini. He was furious because I attributed the origin of Jackie's pillbox hat to Halston, his rival. Cassini took umbrage over Halston's claim to the original design, but Halston's case was the stronger of the two.

The Features editor suggested I treat Cassini to lunch during my upcoming trip to New York. "Add the bill to your expense account," she said. "Let him pick the restaurant."

He picked the Pool Room at The Four Seasons, one of the priciest eateries in Manhattan at the time. He was a regular; the maître d' knew him well. They whispered to one another before the designer strode to the booth where I was seated. As an opening, Cassini leaned in close, fingered the lapel of his sport jacket, and said, "It's cashmere. Just feel it."

I abstained. He urged. I re-abstained. He got the hint.

Throughout the meal, Cassini told tales about Hollywood celebrities he knew, dated, dumped, or been dumped by, including Grace Kelly, famously. All the while, the maître d' kept bringing him cup after cup of tea. At one point, the silver-haired designer asked me if I would like to join him for a weekend at his secluded country home, an ice-white, thirty-five-room Renaissance style mansion on more than forty acres in Oyster Bay Cove, Long Island. I told him I would not.

Back at the Paramount Hotel, I parsed the exorbitant bill, and I smiled. The teacups were not filled with tea. They had contained double shots of Russian vodka.

Readers love Fashion Week stories, but the routine apparel trend pieces I wrote that the *Journal Sentinel* published with pictures of models wearing clothing from Milwaukee stores, well, those pieces brought in advertising, and the higher-ups slathered me with encouraging notes.

Editor #1 – Spectacular spring fashion section.

Editor #2 – Sunday's fashion section was outstanding.

Did these guys just sit through sensitivity training?

Chapter 3
Into the Unknown
September 2001

The cheetahs are back

THE FLIGHT TO LaGuardia leaves on Saturday morning. Well ahead of time, I'm packed and ready to go. I don't want to forget anything important, don't want any surprises while I'm in New York. Everything in the suitcase is black. I learned that lesson the hard way.

The first time I covered Fashion Week, it was the dead of winter. I wore my good wool coat, a cherry red number with a double row of shiny brass buttons. In a universe of head-to-toe black, my scarlet coat got noticed, and not in a good way.

But later that day, I regained a shred of confidence. A bowl of roses was waiting for me at the Paramount Hotel, along with this hand-written note from the most famous designer in America:

Welcome to New York
Ralph

During my years as a fashion writer, I have dabbed my wrists with perfume given to me by Carolina Herrera and powdered my nose with a compact from Evelyn Lauder. I have had supper with a PR gal from Timex who owned a tugboat, eaten breakfast with America's Cup skipper Dennis Conner, and sat to a private brunch with Vera Wang. I whispered a courteous hello to Britain's Prince Andrew, Duke of York, on one of his trips to New York. In return, I received a regal, nearly imperceptible nod. I once sat at a runway show behind Woody Allen and Soon-Yi Previn. I tried to not stare as the famous director and his adopted daughter/lover canoodled. But their relationship was all over the tabloids at that point, and Soon-Yi had chosen to dress for a very public event in a getup that looked remarkably like baby-doll pajamas, so like everybody else, I stared.

Isabella Rossellini invited me to her hotel suite a while back. She was pitching a new line of skincare. We sat side-by-side on a dainty sofa and chatted about lotions and potions. At length, a waiter arrived with lunch.

"I wondered whether you eat meat," Isabella said, "so I ordered portobello."

I do not eat meat. I have never consumed a toadstool and I did not think I ever would. But who could pass up portobello with Isabella?

In New York one winter, I arranged to do a background piece about a new young designer, and in return he gave me a front row seat for his show in the Waldorf's fabled Starlight Ballroom. I arrived early. Presently, Kathy and Rick Hilton slid in next to me. I guess they felt right at home; at the time, the Hilton Group owned the Waldorf. Their daughters, Paris and Nicky Hilton, were just old enough at the time to be the show's celebrity models. For a good twenty minutes, I sat next to Kathy and Rick Hilton in an empty ballroom, and we did not acknowledge each other's existence. I did not, actually, know who they were, so I was hoping they would introduce themselves. Alas, no. Finally, the Hiltons' private-jet friends trickled in. One by one, they bent across me to bestow air kisses upon exalted Hilton cheeks. With intuition instilled during generations of wealth bred to beauty, they, too, ignored me.

On one occasion, I saved the life of Uma Thurman. Well, sort of.

A designer had decided to show his new collection on the top floor of an abandoned warehouse in the Meat Packing District. The organizers had enthroned Uma in the front row, next to a thick support column that served to hide her from banks of photographers at the far end of the cavernous space. But Uma did not go to a trendy fashion show to be unseen. Now and then, she peeked from behind the column and smiled into the cameras. Each time, she yanked a cable that workers had loosely clamped to the column.

I was two rows back. When Uma yanked the cable a third time, I looked up and realized it was a fat electrical cord that provided power to a cannon-sized spotlight mounted high on the column. The canister was directly over Uma's head, and it was wobbling. An Italian guy sat between Uma and me. I knew he was Italian because he had draped a cashmere sweater the color of apricots over his shoulders, and it didn't slide off. I tapped the sweater and warned him Uma was in danger. He merely shrugged. *Non capisce.* I pointed to the canister. He sighed and looked up. Then he *capisced.* In a stream of rapid Italian, he alerted Uma to the danger just as she was about to yank the cable again. She shrugged. Apparently she is not fluent in Italian. The sweater guy pointed. Uma looked up, gasped, and released the cable. Thus was the life of movie star spared.

Most designers put on their shows under great, white tents in Bryant Park, a pocket-sized greensward dotted with mature sycamores and extemporaneous groupings of French folding chairs. From there, it was a short walk to my two favorite hotels, the Paramount on West 46th Street and the Broadway Millennium, across Times Square on West 44th Street.

The Paramount eschews self-promotion. There is no sign out front. A spray of red roses plunked in a container embedded in the limestone façade guides those in the know to the hotel entrance. The guest rooms are the size of a dollhouse closet. But I liked the Paramount's ethos of form over function because it parallels the world of high fashion, and I liked the dark anonymity of the Millennium Broadway.

Each morning, I made my way to Bryant Park and joined a throng of ticketholders assessing one another with quick up-down glances. At some imperceptible signal, we'd file into the maw of the gigantic main tent, shuffling like cows in a chute. During the wait for a show to begin, my reporter friends and I chatted over the low thump of techno-music and tried to identify incoming celebrities, a challenge we dealt with collaboratively.

"Who's that? Is it somebody?"

"Bebe Neuwirth."

"Nah. Julia Louis-Dreyfus."

"Sofia Coppola was at Marc Jacobs last night. Wait, is Hilary Swank down there?"

"I got Ethan Hawke two chairs from Bebe."

"Is Hawke with an 'e'?"

The stage crew finally amped up the music, took the tent to black, and lashed the runway with laser flashes. The lead model glided out, trailed by clones in slightly different ensembles. Each clomped to the end of the runway and back and then disappeared. In an average of seventeen minutes, sixty or seventy models in unwearable and unaffordable outfits raced flat-footed around the runway.

Inevitably, a few rogue designers spurned the sterility of the Bryant Park tents and lured the fashion pack to architectural gems like Grand Central Terminal, to places imbued with history and character like the Apollo Theater, or swanky destinations like the Starlight Room. Edgy designers took us to Depression-era ballrooms or dank, cobblestone plats below bridge abutments, baleful surroundings to highlight sumptuous collections.

I traveled to New York a dozen or more times to cover the runway shows and often the clothes were not the story. Midwest readers liked celebrity sightings, and at Fashion Week there was no shortage of that.

On one of my first assignments to New York, I got on an elevator at the SoHo Grand Hotel and found myself sharing the ride with Isaak Mizrahi. Along the way up, he regaled his staffers with a tale about his mother's holiday cooking. He regaled me right along with them. Isaak Mizrahi is a funny, funny guy.

Early on, I realized that an Anna Wintour sighting at the shows was not unusual, at least at the best of the best shows. I saw her often (from afar) and have concluded that underneath the iconic sunglasses and full-forehead bangs, the editor of *Vogue* is not a funny, funny gal. In fact, I am hard-pressed to recall a single time I ever saw Anna crack a smile during Fashion Week, but I have no idea why that was.

During another New York trip for the paper, I took in the extraordinary sight of Donald Trump dandling his young daughter, Tiffany, on his knee while awaiting the start of a fashion show at which Ivanka was the celebrity model. But the real estate mogul and future United States president was not the only one to tote a tot to the tents. I watched Aerosmith rocker Steven Tyler in full-bore daddy mode, surrounded by his younger children and grinning broadly as his daughter, Liv, walked a runway.

I tried to chat up beautiful Kimora Lee Simmons at a Baby Phat show. She was holding an infant in her arms. It occurred to me that we both are mothers. I figured we had that plus being from St. Louis in common. Actually, I had almost nothing in common with a glamorous six-foot-tall model married to a music mogul urban menswear entrepreneur and worth millions upon millions. I think Kimora sensed that right off. Ours was a momentary conversation.

Whether still in diapers or, er, *back* in diapers, Fashion Week afficionados of every age made their way twice a year to the Bryant Park tents. More than once I watched a frail, stick-thin Brooke Astor hobble from her limousine, negotiate the park steps, and make her way into the tents for an Oscar de la Renta show.

During one of my first trips to New York, Ralph Lauren invited me to his Madison Avenue headquarters for Brazilian coffee and chocolate-dipped strawberries. Okay, me and fifteen or twenty other fashion writers. I was awestruck but sufficiently sentient to inform readers back home about the carpets from Persia, the palm trees potted in Chinese dynasty urns, and equestrian paintings hanging on raised-panel mahogany walls. At the urging of my fashion columnist friends, I made a move to snag an interview with Demi Moore, but she had shown up with jack-booted bodyguards and they blocked me out.

One year, British film star Sarah Miles arrived at a show unaccompanied, maybe even without an invitation. Her career had surged during the 1960s and 1970s, notably with the sweeping film, *Ryan's Daughter.* Perhaps the young house attendants in a tizzy trying to find an empty seat in an overbooked tent weren't familiar with her body of work. Given that she showed no sign of departing gracefully, an usher marched her up the bleachers and indicated that a spot in Row 10, three seats off the aisle, next to a nobody reporter from Milwaukee, was all hers. What could an unrecognized celebrity do but fidget and fume and waggle her hand in the air for further seating assistance? Right before the lights dimmed, one of the show producers plucked her from the Oblivion Section and restored her to an open seat far below, and all was right again in heaven and on earth.

The morning I spent backstage with Bobbi Brown as she daubed products from her line of cosmetics on the flawless faces of Fashion Week models was far more enjoyable. Bobbi was kind and patient and never indicated that she had no idea who I was, or why I had glommed onto her.

As for some of the other celebrities? Gracious, kind, patient? Not so much.

When Carolina Herrera backed out of a benefit appearance in Milwaukee at the last minute, she reneged on a promise to hundreds of Wisconsin women who had paid dearly to fill a rococo ballroom, and who had expected Carolina to join them for lunch and a short runway show. I decided to write it up exactly as I saw it, and eventually I did. In the meantime, something equally juicy came along. Bette Midler happened to be in Milwaukee that day for a performance unrelated to the benefit event in the ballroom. When the frantic organizers of the benefit begged the comedian to fill in for Carolina, or merely take hold of a microphone and say hello to the ladies, she refused. That was okay by me; it wasn't Midler's problem to fix. But later, when I saw Bette running her fingers across clothes hanging in the models' changing room and Herrera's advance man taking notes, I wrote that up, too. Herrera banished me from her next Fashion Week show, and her staff gave me the worst seat in the tents for the following one.

The trio of huge white tents erected every spring and fall in Bryant Park was a magnet for reporters and photographers from around the world. That made the 6th Avenue approach to the park, with it's broad, flat steps and expansive upper landing, an ideal place for up-and-comers to be noticed.

One day, I arrived at the park and saw that a small crowd had gathered near the steps. I moved closer and saw the onlookers were focused on three girls in their early teens, each wearing a party dress of iridescent orange satin. An older woman stood before them, and at her signal they began to sing. It took but a moment to realize the youngsters were incredibly talented, destined for grander stages. The child in the middle, though, was the star. When they finished, someone in the crowd called out, "Hey, what's the name of your group?"

The girl in the middle broke out a radiant smile and said, "Why, we're Destiny's Child."

I made a note of it and then joined the line for the tents. The fashion show was forgettable. The girl who sang like there was no tomorrow, oh, she was memorable. Years later, that child in bright orange satin crossed my mind, and I realized she was Beyoncé Knowles. An impossibly talented child yearning for recognition, a child who would become an international superstar, had performed a free concert that day for anyone on a busy New York Street who cared to listen.

I came to regard a trip to New York as similar to a trip to Hollywood, but with supermodels. Bob Mackie, who famously designed the green velvet *Gone with the Wind* gown for Carol Burnett's television show, punched up a modest walkabout presentation at his studio with an appearance by Angela Lansbury. She mingled amiably with fashion writers whom she would never again see, the epitome of a gracious star of stage, screen, and *Murder, She Wrote.*

Ed McMahon was in fine form at his wife's debut collection. The long-time sidekick of Johnny Carson had ample reason to be comfortable in the limelight, and he was. By then he was not a young man. When he bent his tall frame so he could hear and be heard over the background music, I found myself addressing an impressive set of choppers.

One day during a Fashion Week, I returned to my room at the Paramount to find an engraved invitation to a sunset garden party hosted by Ralph and Ricky Lauren. The party was to take place the following evening on the grounds of the Cooper Hewitt Museum, formerly the Andrew Carnegie mansion.

The evening was gorgeous. The air was soft, the light breeze benevolent. I strolled in the grand entrance with a newspaper friend from California. Our footfalls clicked on the marble floor. Sharp young men wearing tuxedoes and discreet earphones moved us through the building.

"Cheetahs," my friend whispered. "Don't linger."

We hurried down a sweeping staircase to the garden. Waiters bent with trays of fluted champagne, foie gras stuffed figs, and fist-sized strawberries. Arias wafted on night air redolent with the scent of late roses. We mingled, savoring the glamour.

I didn't give a thought to the men who had put up a diaphanous tent at the far end of the garden. Or the electricians who wired crystal chandeliers in the tent. The caterers and furniture haulers. The unseen dressers drizzling gowns over marble-skinned models smoking cigarettes and leafing through *Pravda* in their thong underwear. The stylists fiddling with perfect hair and makeup. Event planners had whisked away every trace of effort.

The music swelled. Ralph beckoned. Ricky moved to his side. Guests ambled to the tent.

"I feel like one of the ancient Romans," I said to a friend as we lowered ourselves onto one of the cream-colored banquettes.

In slow motion, lanky blond-haired models wearing $10,000 gowns the color of milk pranced into view with the perfect cadence of Lipizzans.

It was soon over. Out front, the next wave of reporters was arriving. Caterers were pinching the second batch of figs onto doily-lined trays. Somewhere unseen, stylists were fussing over models stripped to their thong underwear again. The cheetahs invited us to hit the road.

My writer friends and I walked through a back gate and lingered on the sidewalk under a tall tree. I noticed a parrot on a limb that overhung the garden wall behind us. The bird pivoted its head, as if auditing our return to reality. Odd, I thought, a parrot here on 90ᵗʰ Street. I smiled, thinking it was a planned farewell to a magical evening.

"See that?" I said, nudging a friend.

"The parrot? Yeah, Ralph probably found it on some tropical island and had it brought back."

A woman approached us with a slow, shuffling gait. She was stooped, her features obscured under a halo of wild hair. Even from a distance, we smelled her, a musky, damp-basement odor with undertones of piss. A plastic netting sack hung from the crook of her elbow. She kept it close, as if it contained items of immense importance. We stepped aside, but she paused in our midst. One of my friends jotted a message in his notebook and turned the page to me.

For every New York champagne garden party, you get a bag lady.

We moved along. We had deadlines. Behind us, I heard the woman whistle a sharp two-note summons. I turned and saw the bird flap awkwardly to her shoulder. One of its wings hung at an odd angle. Its feathers were patchy, its eyes ringed with crust.

I flagged a taxi and nose-dived into its back seat moments before an Upper East Side society doyenne could do so. My facile move so infuriated her that she removed one of her Christian Louboutin stilettos and whacked its three-inch needle heel on the hood of the taxi. Thrice. As the cab melted into the current of evening traffic, I glanced back. The woman who had paid $1,000 for a pair of shoes was tucking into a waiting taxi. The woman with the parrot had crossed Fifth and was continuing on, into Central Park and the embrace of indifferent night.⁴

Most reporters don't get out-of-town assignments, lunches at the Four Seasons, or invitations to champagne garden parties, but there is a price to pay. It's noticed, the twice-yearly New York trips, the chic hotels and posh parties and celebrity sightings, and the fact that my saucy stories claim prime real estate in the paper. Desk-bound staffers in the Milwaukee newsroom take note. I know that.

What I don't realize is that someone outside the *Journal Sentinel* newsroom was closely monitoring my work. Someone I have never met has been watching what I do, poring over every word I write, keeping track, biding time, waiting to pounce.

Saturday, September 8, 2001

On the Midwest Express flight from Milwaukee to New York, the crew serves a hot breakfast on fine china. The napkins are linen. The seats are Italian leather. The aroma of chocolate chip cookies baked onboard perfumes the cabin air.

Rick, the staff photographer on this trip, is a few rows behind me. I've worked with him before, but not often; Rick doesn't usually do fashion shoots. Also on the plane is a *Journal Sentinel* graphics editor. Weeks ago, Sheila mentioned to me that she would love to do sketches of the runway models at Fashion Week.

"I always have spare tickets to some of the shows," I tell her. "So come. It'll be fun. You never know what to expect."

That Saturday afternoon and evening, we take in three runway shows. At midnight, I answer the last question from the copy desk and fall into bed at the Paramount.

Sunday, September 9, 2001

We're in Harlem. It's Sunday morning and Rick and I are chasing a woman with feathers on her head.

Somebody in the newsroom thought it would be a good idea for us to get photos and quotes while we're here for a feature about African American women and their church clothes.

Rick and I take a taxi to West 138th Street, where the Abyssinian Baptist Church is concluding its Sunday morning service. I've done my homework. The Rev. Adam Clayton Powell and Rev. Martin Luther King Jr. preached here. "Fats" Waller played the organ. Nat "King" Cole and his bride, Maria, exchanged wedding vows here.

Worshipers stream out. No one is wearing a hat with feathers and oversized bows.

Rick tells the taxi driver to cruise the area. A few blocks from the church, we spot a woman making her way toward a housing complex. Her hair has gone to gray. She walks with a limp, as if she needs a new hip. Her dress is a shade of canary yellow that matches a hat topped with magnificent plumage.

The cab pulls to the curb. Rick and I jump out. The woman senses we're following her, and she hastens her pace. We break into a sprint, but we are still a block behind her when she darts between two buildings and out of sight. I stop, hands on knees, trying to catch my breath. Rick continues to the edge of the complex, but he returns moments later.

"Lost her," he says, sounding disappointed.

Scared her, I tell myself. *We ought to be ashamed.*

We cruise the Harlem streets until Rick gets enough pictures for me to wrap a story around. It will be thin on content and quotes. On the way down to Bryant Park, I remember a fashion columnist friend told me about a posh party at Denise Rich's Fifth Avenue penthouse this afternoon. Denise Rich is rich. Veddy. She and her husband, Marc, were friends with former President Bill Clinton. Back in January, on the final day of the Clinton presidency, Bill famously pardoned his financier friend, Marc, who had skedaddled to

Switzerland when he got into legal hot water. Something about taxes and a deal with Iran.

Today, Marc and Denise's daughter, Ilona, is bringing out her first fashion collection, not at Bryant Park but at her mother's penthouse. Rick and I are not on the guest list, but I have the address. When we get to the stately building, a door attendant outfitted for a Gilbert and Sullivan opera asks to see our invitations. Invitations? We might as well turn our pockets inside out. He scowls and waves us off. But around the side of the building, opportunity knocks. Delivery men hauling bags of ice and trays of hors d'oeuvres up to the party have propped a service entrance door open. How convenient. Rick waits for an elevator; I waltz right in and take the stairs two at a time.

Upstairs, a clueless event coordinator invites me to go on through. Just like that, I crash one of the ritziest parties in Manhattan. The Rich's living room is so grand it dwarfs a baby grand piano in a corner. Silk draperies cascade from the high ceiling and puddle beneath windows with panoramic views of Central Park. I count the sofas, lose count, and write "many" in my notebook. I plunk on a white satin loveseat next to somebody important whom I do not know. Turns out, it's hip-hop mogul Russell Simmons, co-founder of Def Jam Recordings and a titan in the music industry. I ask him if the whole penthouse is as fabulous as the room we are in, which I do not know the name of. Living room? Salon?

"No idea," he says, with a tone of finality. The man has figured out I'm nobody.

One of the caterers is more helpful. "This place has seventeen rooms," she says, breathy. "I heard there's even a gym with a hair salon."

My story runs on Monday morning's front page, above the fold, next to the supremely important daily coverage of something, anything, about the Green Bay Packers.

Well, isn't that rich?

Monday, September 10, 2001

Kenneth Cole's morning show is a hot ticket in more ways than one. It's taking place in a huge transparent plastic tent erected in Rockefeller Center, which would be fine except that the September day is already so warm that the interior of the tent feels like a terrarium. As we wait for the first model to appear, the production crew hands out Krispy Kreme donuts, adding a sugar rush to our discomforts.

At noon, Carolina Herrera sends out models in poet blouses and Old Hollywood gowns in Bryant Park. At one o'clock, Betsey Johnson rolls out a sexy collection at Tavern on the Green. Once again, guests swelter under blazing sunshine while models strut their stuff in mob-moll fedoras and

Moulin Rouge corsets. Back at the Paramount, I take a quick shower and then file a story for the bulldog edition.

Before falling into bed for the night, I phone my husband. I cannot remember a day in our marriage when we haven't connected with one another.

I left my family and my job at the *St. Louis Globe-Democrat* to marry Dennis John Fitzpatrick. It was the smartest thing I ever did. He is a good man, a dutiful, diligent, honorable man steeped in Ignatian concepts. The Jesuits did an outstanding job with Dennis. He is steady. I rise, fall, and judder. Tonight, he's in the middle of a business trip just outside of Washington, D.C. He picks up the call. As usual, much of our conversation revolves around Claire and Meg.

Our daughters turned out well despite our occasional fumblings. With a fresh BFA degree in performance from Miami University of Ohio, Claire has settled in Chicago to look for work, find love, and be "discovered." Claire almost never answers her darn phone, so I give up after a half dozen rings. Meg is enjoying a semester of study abroad, a curriculum which emphasizes travel. I satisfy myself with a reread of her latest email.

> Meg – Hi Mom and Dad! Our weekend in Wales was fabulous, very charming, and quaint. We stayed in Cardiff and went to Mass near our hostel. It was Anglican. It lasted an hour and twenty minutes and involved billows of incense and much kneeling.

Each time I am in New York to cover Fashion Week, I keep up with the news back in Wisconsin. And so I know that tomorrow morning the lead story on the front page of the September 11, 2001, *Milwaukee Journal Sentinel* will announce the death of Wisconsin philanthropist Jane Bradley Pettit, heir to the Allen-Bradley industrial fortune.

What I don't know, cannot know, is that by mid-morning readers will forget the tribute to her life.

Chapter 4
Docile / Fury
Spring 2001

My pistol is dainty

I'M STILL SICK. Oh, I'm better. Much better, really. But I'm not entirely well.

No one at the *Journal Sentinel* knows. It's my private issue and I guard it well.

The trouble started back in April with a visit to my parents in St. Louis.

Each time I return to Thornhill, my girlhood home, I am struck by how the subdivision has matured since our house was built in 1960. Even more startling to me is the extent to which my mother and father have aged.

I think of my mother as the tall, slender, athletic woman who bore six children with ease and reared us with calm assurance. Beyond our infancy, she did not cuddle or coddle us; instead, she motivated us to define worthy goals and achieve them through industrious effort. Now, in late life, she is a diminished version of her former self. Degenerative arthritis has contracted her frame, made her lungs breathy, and her demeanor uncharacteristically docile. The cognitive impairment that afflicted her own mother and that now restricts her only sister has come to define her, too.

By the time of my April visit, her decline has advanced markedly. She sits in a sunny corner of the family room and reads the newspaper for hours. She takes short walks and long naps. She isn't baking Bundt cakes anymore—she isn't baking anything. Neither is Dad. They are eighty now, and their health is fragile. Some nights, their dinner is a bowl of lukewarm soup and soda crackers dabbed with peanut butter. I worry one of them will leave a burner glowing on the stove and reduce the house to flinders.

Among his other ailments, Dad suffers from a rare form of lymphoma. Chemotherapy has failed to get it into remission. The treatments and the disease are ravaging him. Watching Mom deteriorate is an added strain.

Purposefully, he keeps his six adult children in the dark about the daily difficulties at Thornhill. Of course, I'm aware that Mom rarely initiates a new topic when we chat on the phone. And I realize she employs a handful of short, memorized responses to give the impression she is following the thread of the conversation when I call.

"How are you doing, Mom?"

"Oh, can't complain."

"What are you guys having for dinner?"

"Oh, you know, same old thing."

On the third morning of my visit last Spring, I fix the kind of breakfast Mom used to turn out on Sundays: bacon and eggs, sliced melon, toast, juice, and coffee. I am washing the dishes when a sharp cry of pain knifes through the house.

Mother!

I drop a soapy plate into the sink and race through the kitchen and back hall to Dad's den. What I see from the doorway stops me cold. Mom is cowering in a leather chair. Dad is standing over her. He's grabbed her by her wrist and he's jabbing something into her fingers, something sharp. There is blood. *What the hell is going on?*

"Dad, stop it! You're hurting her!"

Dad's temper goes back to his boyhood in New York, where frequent schoolyard spats ended with sessions in the principal's office. When he got engaged to the beautiful society girl from St. Louis, his mother warned him to control his anger. He didn't. He couldn't. On the few occasions when one of his children openly challenged his authority, we knew the consequences: a leather-belt spanking that hurt for hours.

Old age and infirmity have put a sharp edge on my father's temper. It comes quicker and darker now. Over the years, Dad never touched Mother in anger, but all of us had heard the verbal abuse. Each time he belittled her in public, I felt helpless and ashamed, and yet I did nothing, said nothing. None of us did. It is a family dynamic that his advanced age and his children's maturity have not erased.

Until now.

Without a thought to the consequences, I shout again, "Stop it, Dad!"

He doesn't answer, doesn't even look up. Instead, he stabs Mom's fingers twice more with one of his diabetes lancets. Each time, she cries out, tries to pull away, and shrinks further into the chair. Bright threads of blood trickle from the tips of her finger to her wrist.

Dad has been dealing with Adult-Onset Type 2 Diabetes for years, checking his blood sugar levels and injecting insulin into his belly. Cinnamon-colored dots line the waistlines of his shirts. Because he never mentions it, I haven't given it much thought. I doubt my siblings have, either.

I do now.

"What are you doing?" I shout again, heart pounding.

He grits his teeth. In the stunned silence that follows, I realize he's trying to test Mom's blood sugar. But why?

For several long beats, the only sound is my mother's whimpering sobs. Then Dad jabs the lancet into her again.

I move between them, so close I feel his breath on me.

"You're hurting her," I say, locking eyes with him. "Knock it off."

Shaking with anger and indignation, he glares at me. Finally, he hisses, "Get out!"

My father's fury roars over me, hot, fierce, and sour as bile.

I stagger into the hall, horrified. Has my father ordered me to leave the room or to leave Thornhill? How can that be? It's unthinkable.

Reeling with shock and uncertainty, I run up to my old bedroom and pace the floor, catastrophizing.

Dad didn't mean I should leave the room. He meant I should leave the house. Leave Thornhill. Kicked out of my childhood home. I'll never again see my mother, never speak to her, never see my father either, never be able to put things to right, never forget this day, never, ever get over this and it's all my fault, it's all his fault, it's my fault, his fault, my fault.

I dial Dennis at his office. No answer. I call Tom and then Ken, my brothers who live nearby. Both calls go to voicemail. In despair, I leave messages everywhere, throw my clothes into a suitcase, and phone for a taxi. With the door open a crack, I listen for sounds downstairs. Nothing.

From an upstairs window, I watch for the taxi. When it pulls up the long drive, I collect my suitcase and go down to the foyer. I don't see Dad. I presume he's still in his den. I know he hears me, though. If he would only come out to the hall, we could talk and somehow get past this. But he doesn't. Vomit gurgles in my throat.

Mom is waiting for me in the living room. She wraps her arms around me, and I enfold her in mine. She is short now, a hunched and delicate woman who once swam laps in an icy spring-fed pool, hung wet sheets on a line, and ran her teenage sons into the ground on the sunny tennis courts of Thornhill Estates.

She cries into my shoulder. I hold her for perhaps the last time and weep silent, bitter tears.

The taxi driver honks, and I stiffen. Mom begs me to stay, tells me she's all right, says it was nothing, it doesn't hurt. Please stay, Cathy. Please don't leave like this.

Mother is devastated at the thought of me leaving. I am heartbroken at the prospect of never seeing her again.

"I can't stay, Mom. You know it," I tell her. "Come with me, please. Come live with Dennis and me in Milwaukee."

She will not. She will not leave her husband. Not leave her home. I know this. My offer is impulsive, and her reasons are valid enough. She is old, sick, tired, drained, and vulnerable. Newness frightens her. She is a woman of abiding faith, and the wedding vows she made in 1945 compel her lifelong fidelity. And she loves him.

I glance at her hand. It's still bleeding a little. I tell her that Dad is quicker than ever to fly into a rage. I ask her how her children can be sure she will be safe. She takes a step back and shakes her head, and I accept that she will never go. Numb with misery, I take a last look down the empty center hall. Not a sound. Not a footfall.

During the taxi ride to Lambert St. Louis Airport, I slump against the seat, emotionally shattered by my mother's physical and cognitive decline, by my father's worsening illness, his flashes of anger, his rough treatment of her, and the horrible thought that barely an hour after her husband pierced her fingers with a lancet and drew blood, I walked out on her.

I cannot forgive myself for that.

That afternoon at home, I take a long, warm shower. On the way to the laundry room I stop cold. The shoulder of the blouse I wore this morning is streaked with my mother's blood.

In the following weeks, I replay that jarring morning at Thornhill a hundred times in my mind, unaware of the toll it is taking.

> Editor – Hi Catherine. Hope you survived your trip in one piece.
>
> Catherine – Flying back to MKE today. I'll see you in the newsroom tomorrow.

Such a breezy answer, as if nothing's wrong. Nothing at all.

Back at work, I organize my notes from the Texas trip. The Death Row story and photos will run large and ultimately take a major award. Winning any competition is validating for a newspaper writer, but in prestige, one award dwarfs the rest. In 1997, not long after the merger, editors nominated my fashion columns for a Pulitzer Prize in Journalism. The $5,000 prize is given for a "distinguished example of feature writing giving prime consideration to high literary quality and originality." Although I did not even come close to winning a Pulitzer, the nomination felt fantastic.

Now, though, my primary focus is an overwhelming fear that I will never see my parents again, never hear their voices, never be welcome at Thornhill, never be invited to family reunions, never again be regarded as a member of the family I love.

I slog through the days engulfed in hopelessness. I cry too much, sleep too much, have trouble being productive at work. Nothing seems to me to be worth the effort of doing it. Laundry piles up. Dishes languish in the sink. Days pass before I think to shampoo my hair.

Until now, I never thought much about the importance of hope. I took for granted the belief that something better is right around the corner. I do not regard myself as a particularly perky person, though others might. But until the late Spring of 2001 I had never felt so hopeless and despairing. Gradually, I realize that whatever is wrong with me is smothering my motivation and making me feel disconnected from those I love. I begin to question my worth to them. If my own father can kick me out of his life impulsively, would it be just as easy for my husband to do so? For my children?

In the wee hours, I wake from nightmares and wonder if I am dispensable. Soon, I convince myself that no one will miss me if I'm gone. From there, it is a short step to mulling over ways to dispose of myself.

After work, I always take the highway home. It's about a ten-minute drive. One day in May, my gaze flickers from the highway to the dashboard and then to my hands. I sample what it feels like to let go of the steering wheel and see how quickly the car would drift into another lane, or farther. I envision giving the wheel a yank to the left, envision feeling my car leave the pavement and rumble into the low, grassy swale that separates northbound traffic from vehicles heading south. It occurs to me that if I press hard on the accelerator, my car will continue across the median and into the southbound lanes, perpendicular to onrushing traffic. And that would be that.

Dissembling at sixty miles an hour, I consider my alternatives. I could yank the steering wheel to the right instead, sideswipe a northbound car speeding along next to me. Then both cars would spin like tops onto the shoulder. If all went well, my car would land upside-down. Maybe even explode.

Must remember to fill the tank.

Once, I lift my fingertips from the wheel and count to eight before I come to whatever common sense I have left. On some level, I realize it's a horrid thing I'm contemplating, one that would take the occupants of another car along on my disastrous last ride.

Okay, so death by car crash is out.

That's when the gun appears.

One morning in early June, the image of a pistol flashes across my field of vision and quickly vanishes. I hate guns, loathe them, never owned one and never will, but I don't obsess about briefly seeing a gun when no gun is actually there. But I'm mildly surprised when it happens again the following day. After that, I begin to look forward to a return appearance.

The pistol, *my* phantom pistol, is dainty. It's the type of weapon Old West madams tucked into garters underneath their cheap satin gowns. Mine is sterling silver, though, with scrollwork etched into its slender barrel. The grip is ivory or mother of pearl, a work of art. It doesn't occur to me to blink it away, which is odd because—and I can't stress this enough—I have a visceral aversion to guns. But for some reason, my phantom gun is mesmerizing to me.

Soon, it's making daily appearances. Even to me, it's clear something is wrong. I phone a friend who is a therapist, and she connects me with a psychiatrist.

Dr. Donna is kind and soft-spoken. At the end of the first appointment, she says she thinks I am depressed. She prescribes diazepam and weekly appointments. After a few sessions, she changes my medication to amitriptyline, and I start to improve. In mid-June, I work up the courage to dial my parents' phone number. Dad answers. After a startled pause (on both ends), we manage to patch the breach between us.

How's the weather down there, Dad?

Oh, not too bad.

But our relationship, once close and warm, is wary, held together under a veneer of light conversation. We both know it. After a couple of minutes, Dad turns the phone over to Mother.

I assume, because I know no differently, that depression is my problem. It is the focus during my therapy sessions with Dr. Donna. I do not realize there is an overarching illness at work here, and that depression is only part of the it.

The common belief is that depression is about crying, but it goes deeper than that. In my case, it began the day my father abruptly ejected me from his den and worsened as weeks passed with no contact between us. At first, I assumed the crying spells and suppurating sadness would diminish on their own. How foolish I was to sink to the brink of despair before I realized I needed professional help. Who knows? Maybe with depression, that's normal.

Throughout the summer of 2001, I see Dr. Donna every week and take the antidepressant as prescribed. By late August, I am convinced I have shaken off my despondence.

But the overarching issue is not depression, it is Post-Traumatic Stress. And I have not shaken it off, merely tamped it down.

> Catherine – Claire, I believe you have absconded with my TWA frequent flier miles.

> Meg – London is not at all what I expected. Everything is old.

> Claire – As for the job search, I'm trying. I'm applying everywhere that I can, and I'm going through four agencies. I'm bummed out. I filed for unemployment. I'm going to need the money. Thank God I have supportive friends and family.

No one but Dr. Donna knows about my phantom pistol or about the dangerous episodes of dissembling in the car. I cannot bear to confide in Dennis. He would never understand. Besides, he is not a fan of overt emotion. If he knew, he'd worry; we can't have both of us falling apart.

At work, I steel myself to hide my symptoms from everyone except Michele, my friend from our days together in the *Sentinel's* Features Department. Michele can keep a confidence. Even so, I hold back details from her.

Journalists are expected to be vigorously inquisitive, to pursue stories with energy, curiosity, impartiality, and verve. Metro daily reporters do not mope around their newsrooms, languishing in despair and self-pity, not the good reporters, not the ones who get meaty assignments and trips to Fashion Week.

I want to go to New York again, badly. I love my job, and covering runway shows in Manhattan is a huge part of the job. Besides, it's a terrific opportunity to write creatively. And it's so darn fun. Gliding around Manhattan to runway shows and popping in on after-parties transports me to a glittering universe few experience firsthand.

By late August, I'm confident I have recovered enough to manage the stresses of deadline reporting from New York City. I've done it before. I'm ready. I know what's ahead.

I have no idea what's ahead.

Chapter 5
A Gonzo Reporter
1971-73

A foot in the door

MY GRANDFATHER WAS a commanding presence, heir to a successful family-owned furniture manufacturing company. Tall and trim, he swept his fair hair back from a high forehead, had his nails professionally manicured, and showed up at our backyard barbecues in bespoke sport jackets and Italian shoes buffed to a high shine. My sister and I once peeked into his closet, and I discovered items so puzzling I had no name for them. With syrupy patience, my sister said, "jodhpurs and opera pumps, dummy." In his later years, when he flew off to hunt big game in Canada or to reel in marlin off the coast of Mexico, he dispatched our grandmother to a health spa somewhere in the South, a place of stark simplicity, rigorous exercise, and starvation provisions from which she returned thinner, somewhat.[5]

His name was Arthur J. Meier, but my sister and brothers and I were instructed to refer to him as A.J. Other than that, he did not encourage informality and we dared not test his tolerance for it. He was not a grandpa, not the kind of man to bounce a baby on his knee. But on special occasions, if Pam and I were well-scrubbed, dressed in velvet, and on our best behavior, we detected vague indications that our existence pleased him. In time, he paid for Pam and me to spend summers at elite equestrian camps near the Canadian border. And, later, he paid our first two years' college tuition, room, and board. Pam started at Marquette University and then transferred to the University of Missouri's journalism school.

In hindsight, I think our grandfather had expected her to aim higher—Smith or Vassar perhaps—on the theory that his generosity would lead to a more refined and prosperous life than she or I might otherwise have had. But I do not regret choosing to go to Creighton.

At an off-campus party during Freshman Welcome Week, a stick-skinny guy caught my eye. Or rather, his mismatched clothes did—tight navy and white striped jeans that barely grazed his ankles and a short-sleeved, oxford cloth, button-down shirt.

Sheesh, somebody get this guy help! Who is he, anyway?

Dennis.

After a virulent cocktail (and perhaps two), I told him I could no longer feel my teeth. It was the start of a seven-year courtship and a till-death-do-us part marriage. Dennis was fun and funny, courtly in an old-fashioned way, and smart. He tutored me to a final grade of C+ in World Civilization, an accomplishment I celebrated by setting my notes on fire in the sink of my dorm room.

Creighton c. 1968

Toward the end of my sophomore year at Creighton, I faced a crossroad: wait for a financial miracle, or transfer to a less costly school. It had been my habit to write to my older sister every now and then, and I did my best to make each letter to her a literary gem. When she finally answered, it was just two lines on a postcard, but those few words changed my life:

"Hey kid, you can write. Why don't you come on over?"

I smiled when I read my sister's card, as if I finally could see the path to a job that was exciting, worthwhile, and achievable. Not a job, a career, one that would forever change my life.

Although I was heartbroken to leave Dennis, I quickly fell in love with Mizzou and with journalism. Covering stories for the *Columbia Missourian* felt meaningful, even the dreadful rural electrification committee meetings. Some days I never wanted college to end. Other days I couldn't wait to start my career.

In journalism school I heard stories about a gonzo reporter named Kate Webb. She was just seven years older than me, an earthy Australian who smoked and drank and did not shrink from danger. In a subset of reporting dominated by men at the time, she was soft-spoken and too pretty. But there was trauma in her past—a close friend's suicide, both parents killed in a car crash—the kind of trauma that can change a person in profound ways. While still in her mid-twenties, Kate bought a one-way plane ticket to Ho Chi Minh City, then known as Saigon, and badgered the UPI bureau chief so relentlessly for a job that he finally let her fill in when his regular war correspondents were not available. Before long, she was filing gripping dispatches from the jungle.

During my senior year at Missouri University, North Vietnamese troops captured Kate near Phnom Penh, in Cambodia. The soldiers tortured, starved, and bound her with p'dou vines. Then they tossed her in an earthen hole. Days later, a burned, bullet-ridden body was found and assumed to be Kate. *The New York Times* ran her obituary. But after twenty-four days in captivity, Kate Webb stumbled out of the jungle, ten pounds lighter, but alive.[6]

I idolized her. I wanted to be a war correspondent like Kate. I wanted to run toward danger and bring out news of conflict, desperation, and consequence. I was young and romantically inclined, untested as a journalist and unaware of the harsh reality of such a job. Clueless.

I graduated in June of 1971, propelled into a stagnant economic market. I was lucky to get one job offer and smart enough to grab it. I did not buy a one-way plane ticket to anywhere. I bought a hunter green Mercury Capri and drove it to Hannibal, to a $95-a-week job as a cub reporter for the daily *Hannibal Courier-Post.* I rented the back room of a century-old Queen Anne house, reported little of value from the police blotter, and struggled through a couple of dates with the local heart-throb, an assistant pharmacist whose best asset was his lemon yellow Corvette.

As a cub reporter at the *Courier-Post,* I checked each morning for news at city and county government offices. In the afternoons, I wrote feature stories. On Christmas Eve, I asked for a raise and got all of $1.50 a week extra. At that, I gave two weeks' notice.

Back in St. Louis, the *Globe-Democrat* took me on as a copyeditor. Suddenly, I was at a big city daily. I leased an apartment in a trendy St. Louis suburb, bought a snappy red MG convertible, and refreshed my wardrobe. Life was grand.

Almost.

I was four hundred miles from Dennis, who was in his hometown of Milwaukee slogging through law school. And although I was on the staff of a major newspaper, I was composing headlines, fixing commas, and repairing someone else's mangled grammar, not reporting, not writing.

I developed an eye tic. I lost all perspective about how many shoes I could afford. Finally, I started to freelance stories for the independent *St. Louisan Magazine.* When my work made the magazine's cover for the second month in a row, I knew I had the ammunition to jumpstart my stalled writing career. I marched into the office of the *Globe's* managing editor and thwapped a copy of the magazine on his desk.

"I want to write," I barked at him.

The man did not look up. He simply slid the magazine to the side and returned his attention to the sports pages. I had overstepped.

Three weeks later, though, I was writing feature stories and covering the education beat at the *Globe.* Each evening after the first edition deadline, I joined two newsroom friends at the St. Louis Press Club for a bourbon Old Fashioned and a cup of warm rice pudding. I dated guys with varying degrees of interest (on both sides) and waited for Dennis to finish law school and propose.

From the beginning, I knew no one would ever love me as deeply as Dennis John Fitzpatrick. That I was astute enough to realize it is fortunate, for I loved him, too. Dearly.

We were married in St. Louis on a cold, damp morning in November of 1974. After the honeymoon, we returned to Milwaukee to make a life together. Our first apartment was blocks from his childhood home. It was 395 miles from mine.

I was confident I would sail into a reporting job at one of Milwaukee's daily newspapers. The *Sentinel* swatted me away. I scored an interview at the *Milwaukee Journal,* but it went badly. The editor asked to see the list of proposed feature stories I had brought along. I handed it over, and he kept it. In the coming months, I waited for a phone call that never came, and I saw my ideas appear as stories under the bylines of various *Journal* staffers. Lesson learned.

My father-in-law, a retired vice-president of Wisconsin Bell Telephone Company, arranged a job for me in the utility's public relations department. Now and then, my boss let me wax poetic with an adjective.

It seemed like the perfect time to get pregnant, and I did. Twice. While I was home full-time with our two little girls, I freelanced stories for the *Journal* and the *Sentinel.* Each time, it reminded me how I loved to write.

In 1987, the *Sentinel's* features editor offered me part-time work, and I jumped at the opportunity. I was confident that soon I would be writing important stories, consequential stories, even a story about a once-in-a-lifetime event that changed the world.

By the time of the merger in 1995, I had been a part-time home writer and shopping columnist at the *Sentinel* for years. On the day I was called to a glass office on the perimeter of a newsroom on high alert, I realized the editor had already decided my professional future. What I did not know was this:

On a sunny September day in New York, the type of reportage I had fantasized about in journalism school, a fierce, breaking story Kate Webb would have covered, would be mine.

Chapter 6
Dawn
September 11, 2001

The sky is blue as glacier ice

AT 6:32 A.M., the sun crests the rooftops of Long Island. Its rays gild steak-knife ripples on the East River. Glassy buildings glint in the early light. Strands of bulbs scalloping the bridges wink off. The city wakes.

The sky is blue as glacier ice, the air heavy with the scents of coffee, cigarettes, perfume, bus fumes, sunflowers in bunches, river water.

For more than eight million New Yorkers across the five boroughs, the day begins routinely enough. Driven by obligation, necessity, arrogance, ambition, or desire, they walk out into the crystalline September day. Among them is a receptionist with frosted hair. A janitor with a wife and kids. A third-generation firefighter. A doctor with a headache. A bond trader with an eye tic. A police officer whose lawn needs mowing. A grandmother whose dog is sick. An accountant with tickets to a show. A busboy who sings at church.

By noon, 2,977 men, women, and children will have vanished into thin air.

Chapter 7
Professional Responsibilities
7 a.m. September 11, 2001

How ya doin today?

IN ROOM 801 at the Paramount Hotel, I scan the Fashion Week schedule and plot the day ahead. In Bryant Park, I expect staffers will soon roll carts of bagels, coffee, and champagne into the press area.

The first runway show is a wedding gown collection. Meh, skippable. The next six are not optional. I steel myself for a day in which I will rush to shows, take notes, rush back to the hotel, and write, write, write. At midnight, I'll order room service eggs and take a late spell-check call from the copy desk.

"Shouldn't that be Donna ka-RAN with two r's?"

Um, no. One will suffice.

It's all good. I feel great. I'm lucky to be here—I didn't exactly put in a stellar effort at work this past summer. It's time I stopped letting the problems of my parents interfere with my professional responsibilities.

I tell myself that, and yet I woke this morning in a hotel room in Midtown Manhattan at the beginning of Fashion Week, reliving for the ninety-ninth time the scene in my father's den.

And I cannot fathom why Dad continues to let Mom drive, except that age has dimmed his judgment. One day last fall, she backed her Cadillac out of the garage and drove to Straub's, a small grocery store about two miles from Thornhill. Mom and Dad are frequent customers; the store employees know them by name. That day, Mom bought a few things, put the sack of groceries on the back seat of her car, and vanished. After an hour or so, Dad drove his Jeep to Straub's, saw Mom's car, and went into the store to retrieve her.

"Mrs. Underhill left a long time ago," the manager said, frowning with worry. "Isn't she home by now?"

They searched the store and parking lot. Then they called the police. After a short, terrifying interlude, one of the officers spotted her. She had walked across Clayton Road to Concordia University's sprawling campus. For years, the school's winding lanes were familiar to her; she had walked them often. Later, the officer noted in his report that she was tired, thirsty, and thoroughly lost.

Throughout the spring and summer, Dennis kept me grounded with his enduring love and quiet ministrations. And every email and visit from Claire and Meg reminded me of how buoyant life is when you're young and (almost) carefree. Claire is working part-time jobs in Chicago, going to auditions, and hoping a Broadway producer or Hollywood casting agent will discover her. Meg is a sophomore at the University of Notre Dame, enjoying a semester in London.

> Claire – hello mom, I'm fine. I'm in a fairly good mood today. I have a pretty nice weekend planned. How ya doin today? Plugging along? Working on any cool stories? Luv, c-bear
>
> Catherine – Girls! How are youse guys? Haven't heard in ages. Well, days. Well, hours. But it seems like ages.
>
> Claire – Mom, sometimes I get in trouble if I check my email too many times in one day. Besides, I just had, like, an hour-long conversation with you on Sunday. Sheesh.
>
> Catherine – How blessed I am with beautiful daughters. Thank you for your heartening messages. I always need my family, and especially now. My parents have been a huge and active part of my life, and their old age and infirmities have hit especially hard. Trying to keep up a creative career and 400-mile commutes to St. Louis has been a challenge.

Chapter 8
Cataclysm
Morning, September 11, 2001

A fearsome tempest

THE DIN OF morning rush is reaching a crescendo. Horns honk. Brakes screech. Pedestrians chat on cell phones in languages from Portuguese to Brooklynese. Drivers clip the corners, narrowly missing pedestrians who respond with ripe vocabulary.

I buy a blueberry muffin and coffee at the Dean & Deluca café next to the hotel and then stroll the sidewalk. A bus lumbers along, leaving a slipstream of fumes. A metal utility disc in the pavement plinks like a xylophone under the wheels of a self-important SUV. A cement truck twirls its great belly, making a sound like pennies jiggled in a jar.

8:46:40 a.m.[7]

Almost four miles south of the Paramount, American Airlines Flight 11 with ninety-two souls on board slashes into the North Tower of the World Trade Center. Liquid fire engulfs the interior of the building from the 93rd to the 99th floors.[5] Flames explode from shattered windows. Black smoke billows the air, pours up stairwells, and fills elevator shafts. At the moment of impact, almost 9,000 men and women are inside the tower.

8:48 a.m.

Back in the hotel room, I open my laptop computer and turn on *The Today Show*. On the television screen, a small box shows a soaring white skyscraper. Smoke is bursting from a jagged hole in the tower.

I dial the *Journal Sentinel* switchboard. No answer. I call an editor at home. She picks up immediately.

"It's Catherine. There's a big fire in a tall building here. Think I should cover it?"

Her television is on. She is seeing what I'm seeing.

"Go," she says. Then louder, urgently, "Go! GO!"

I call Rick's room. He's already talked with one of the photo editors.

"Meet me in the lobby in five minutes," Rick tells me. "If you're not there, I can't wait."

I fill a tote bag with everything I think I'll need for a few hot hours on the streets: press credentials, notebooks, pens, a cell phone, Kleenex, a bottle of water, my driver's license, a credit card, and $100 in cash.

I don't think to phone Dennis. It's just a fire. I'll be back to the runway shows by noon. I don't call Claire or Meg or my parents. Failing to do so is one of my most bitter regrets.

9:03:11 a.m.

Flight 175 slams deep into the South Tower like a bullet shot from a rifle. The fireball consumes the 77th to the 85th floors. Black smoke roars out the gaping impact hole. In a single second, six hundred people are either killed or trapped.

Unaware of the second attack, Rick and I sprint the few blocks from the hotel to Times Square and flag a cab.

9:14 a.m.

Broadway is at a standstill. The voice of a dispatcher crackles over the taxi's dashboard radio. He says the fire downtown is raining debris onto nearby streets. He says it's a mess; motorists are walking away from their cars, leaving them in the street. The gridlock is going viral. I peer out the taxi's front window. Although we are too far to see anything, I realize the fire downtown is a big story. I twist to look out the back window. The Times Square zipper, that enormous scrolling display of illuminated headlines, is reporting earlier events, news the world will soon forget. I take out a notebook and pen. That's what will lead my news story.

9:18 a.m.

Rick and I realize we can't sit in Midtown traffic forever. After I pay the driver, we run to the nearest subway station and get on a southbound train seconds before the doors close.

9:32 a.m.

At the 14th Street/Eighth Avenue station, the train hisses to a stop. We expect the doors to glide open. They don't. I glance at the other passengers in the train car. Fissures of tension crease their faces. Mine, too, I expect. With good cause: We are in a closed train car filled with commuters under the streets of New York, stalled in a labyrinthine passage dug with shovels and pickaxes a century ago.

For eleven minutes, we stay where we lay.

9:37:06 a.m.

Flight 77 plows into the Pentagon building in Virginia.

9:43 a.m.

The train doors open.

Rick and I join a throng of commuters climbing ziggurat stairs, heading for daylight. Behind us, the station is oddly silent. No tokens clinking. No turnstiles ratcheting. No violin solos. New York has remanded custody of its subway stations to the rats.

I blink into blazing daylight and realize we're still a long way north of the World Trade Center. I know that the North Tower has been burning for an hour, and I've heard rumors that a plane has hit the South Tower, but I have no confirmation about it. And no idea that a third attack plane has speared into the Pentagon, or that the passengers and crew of a fourth plane are in grave danger over Pennsylvania.

Rick and I hike south and a little westerly. With few cars, taxis, and trucks on the streets and avenues, the city should be quiet as a church. We should be able to hear air conditioners droning in the windows of pre-war apartments, cats meowing on Greenwich Village stoops, bodega clerks humming as they stack pears in bins out front. The streets and avenues should be as quiet as country lanes.

They are not.

A cacophony of chaos and fear is rewriting the symphonic score of New York. The air is charged with the pulsing sound of crisis. Fire engines broadcast long baritone blasts and deafening honks. Police sirens speed up and down the octaves. Ambulances wail a distinctive two-note warning reminiscent of the London Blitz. Sirens ululate across the harbor to Lady Liberty, race the halls of Ellis Island, and meld with the foghorns of tour boats churning back to piers. Peril rings incessantly in the ears of a city painfully aware it is under attack. I wonder, when the sirens finally fall silent, will the silence fall fierce on the ear?[8]

At the triangle at Hudson and Bleeker, we join about forty people facing south, staring in awe at an appalling sight. From here, the upper levels of the North Tower and part of the South Tower are visible. Both are pushing columns of thick, black smoke into the perfect day.

There is no doubt now; this is a huge story. I write a single word in my notebook.

Thunderstorm

At the West Side Highway just south of the Chelsea Piers, I get a clear view of the upper floors of the North Tower. Of its symmetric verticals. Of its elegant simplicity. And of the lurid orange gash that marks the impact site, like the rictus grin on a Halloween pumpkin. Fire is working its way up and down the floors. Helicopters swarm, veer close, and angle off. At first, I'm shocked. *Why the hell aren't they rescuing people from the rooftops?* Then I realize the thick smoke makes a roof landing impossible. My stomach churns at the thought of the cataclysm inside the towers.

Car radios blare updates into the streets, bulletins that mix rumor with fact and fear. Security agents have evacuated the White House! The Pentagon is attacked! The government has effectively sealed the United States!

9:59:04 a.m.

Pierced, burned, gutted, and structurally crippled, the 1,362-foot South Tower sucks itself inward and falls, vanquished by men in the name of their god. The tower stood for twenty-nine years. Mortally wounded, it held together for fifty-six minutes, even as its structural steel melted. As the world watches in horror, it vanishes from the skyline in eleven seconds.

A massive cloud of debris fountains down, obliterating everything clustered at the tip of Manhattan.

The destruction of so much physical matter roars over the lower city, taking down nearby buildings by the dozens. It paints windows a sickening shade of yellow-brown. It sticks to stop signs and trash receptacles and autumn leaves on spindly city trees. It coats sidewalks. It frosts men and women running for dear life. It clings to their hair, settles on their shoulders, paints their faces, makes them appear otherworldly.

The collapse vaporizes every single person in the tower. It buries every would-be savior who rushed from safety to peril, to a lobby door that marked the threshold between life and death.

The morning is windless, and yet fine particles of debris from America's vanquished tower swirl across oceans, mountains, and continents, circling the marbled world in a fearsome tempest of change. But the abominations of the day are not over.

For those watching on televisions and computer screens from Tulsa to Tel Aviv, the sight of it, even in miniature, jams the senses. For those here, gaping in horror, the instant disappearance of a 110-story skyscraper collapsing from roof deck to lobby, a tower with a skeleton of steel seated on pilings sunk to bedrock, erases every faculty of perception but sight.

During the eleven seconds it takes for the South Tower to thunder into and onto itself, I hear only the faintest sound: a gritty, pebbled noise similar to play-yard sand sifted through a kitchen colander. My wistful out-breath joins the sighs of people near me, a collective human soughing at the sheer sorrow of the thing.

Bathed in morning sunlight, pinned to a highway emptied of traffic, I slump alongside strangers in a world that has crossed over from the existential to the surreal, a helpless observer to a mythic event beyond comprehension. Thoughts swizzle and spin away as I stare at the void where the South Tower was and see it still, its thin, bleached verticals rising as before in parallel perfection. It is nothing, a ghostly afterimage, like the lingering sight of a spent sparkler on a Fourth of July night.

I do not for a single second consider returning to the hotel. I do not regard myself as being in danger. I regard myself as a reporter for a major American newspaper. I regard myself as the only reporter for that newspaper at the scene. I regard myself as a seasoned journalist and as a facile describer. I regard myself as being in the right place at the right time to report a major breaking news event. What I do not think about is the possibility of danger to me. Or how my husband might react when he learns that I chose to leave the safety of the hotel and immerse myself in chaos, fear, and death in the streets. I do not think about how emotionally fragile I had been for the past four months. I do not give a thought to Kate Webb.

In the adrenaline rush of the moment, I do not think beyond the five words I am writing in one of the two reporter's notebooks I brought from the hotel:

Horrified
Armageddon
People
Dumbstruck
Crying

I close the notebook but keep the pen handy. For a long moment, I am numb, held in place by shock and disbelief, barely able to absorb the enormity of what has happened.

The roar of the collapse gives way to silence. Clouds of pulverized concrete, gypsum, glass, paper, wood, plastic, flesh and bone boil into the air. Rivers of people hike north, fleeing up the middle of avenues, pausing to step aside for an oncoming fire truck or speeding ambulance. They shuffle along in a daze, as if they have forgotten their destination but don't care. They march with the purposeful gait of dread, head well forward of the body, suit jacket slung over a shoulder, handbag held to the chest, briefcase slapping a thigh with each long, quick stride. They punch cellphones, hoping for a connection. Perspiration dots their foreheads. Sweat darkens half-circles under their arms.

I try to call the newsroom. No connection.

"It's the antennas," a man says, elbowing past. "They were on the roof."

Rick and I start to run toward the remaining tower. Each time I pause to make an entry in my notebook, I fall a little farther behind. He can shoot pictures and move on faster than I can do interviews and move on. Rick doesn't want to be slowed, and I can't do my job if I'm rushed. We agree to separate.

10 a.m. to 10:16 a.m.

Choppers whir overhead, dip, rise again, and angle off in what must be crushing decisions for the pilots. The streets are beaded with abandoned cars, trucks, buses, bikes, skateboards, dogs, empty baby carriages. Sirens by the dozens still blare as emergency vehicles roar down avenues and traverse through congested cross streets. Men and women in business clothes continue to stream out of buildings and fan out across the urban grid on foot, heading home in mid-morning.

A young woman twists the cap off a bottle of Evian water and takes a long drink. I glance at her. My water is gone. She offers hers. I take a long swig and return it. We conduct the exchange without a word. Neither of us has bothered to wipe the top.

It's that kind of day.

The air is acrid. The street signs are unreadable, covered with dust. On my own now, I head south toward the disaster site. My pulse is a high hum in my ears. The city looks off-kilter to me, stretched like the image in a fun-house mirror. The helicopters have left. Fighter jets scream across the crenelated skyline.

"Are they ours?" a woman asks.

I cast a blank look in her direction.

How would I know? For me, reality is tilting a degree off true.

I need to get a call through to the newsroom, but it takes strategizing. When I see someone talking on a cell phone, I do the praying hands thing and then wave a $50 bill. People end their calls, hand me their phones, and wait while I dictate brief updates to the paper in Milwaukee. But a bodega cashier deftly slips the cash into the pocket of her apron before she waves me to a land-line phone at the rear of the shop. I sit on a carton of Sprite and dial the newsroom. Before I hang up, I ask the newsroom clerk to phone Claire in Chicago and my parents in St. Louis, and to try to reach Dennis. Let them know I'm okay. I am sure that an international call to Meg would never go through, so I don't ask the clerk to try.

Before continuing on, I pause to collect my thoughts. Barely an hour ago, a great winged beast screeched across the harbor and snuffed away a skyscraper, burned it to cinders, reduced it to rubble. For 10,399 days, it stood alongside its mirror image, dominating the skyline of Manhattan. For now, the wounded twin fights on.

Waves of emergency vehicles blare warnings as they race to the desperation at the foot of Manhattan, bearing rescuers who surely know in their thrumming hearts that any soul in the North Tower above the gash is beyond hope.

I am one-half block from the West Side Highway when I see a truck pull to the curb. The truck is cherry red. Ladders, axes, and a coiled white hose cling to its side, held fast by brackets that flash in the sun. FDNY firefighters jump off and head for an egg-shaped public telephone kiosk.

The first man jabs the keypad with trembling fingers; the others fish their pockets for coins. They make sure to keep their backs to the plume down the way, rising like steam from a lava flow.

The firefighter shouts into the receiver. A bear of a man, his voice is high and thin.

"Hi, babe. Put Mikey on the phone."

Pause.

"Go get Mikey!"

I open a notebook. The tragedy downtown is beyond description. Here, the pathos is discrete.

One second. Two. He grinds the receiver into his forehead. In my notebook I write the time, the street intersects, and the numbers painted in gold on the side of the truck.

I turn to the other guys standing in a small circle.

"How are you?" I ask, a ridiculous question but an opening.

I wait as they consider the question and then look away with darting eyes, wring tension from knotted shoulders, try to describe conflicting emotions and fall silent.

"Afraid?"

Sure, he says. They're afraid of secondary attacks, of a bomb. They're ready to do their job, he adds, but they don't want to be victims.

I scribble his words. When I look up, the men are hiking up to the truck, clamping chin straps, checking jacket toggles, twisting wedding rings.

I give them a dry smile. They don't see.

I signal two thumbs up. They don't see.

The driver accelerates. The men stare into the middle distance, at their boots, their friends, anywhere but the ash cloud whirling a skyscraper into the air, a monster coil that contains steel beams and glass windows, elevator shafts and offices, hallways and cubicles, all gone to dust.

More.

Cell phones, keyboards, and coffee cups. Armani neckties, Nike sneakers and Fossil watches, dollar-store socks and Ferragamo high heels. Pennies in purses. Pictures of dimpled babies in desktop frames.

Still more.

The last earthly remains of bond traders and sous chefs, of mothers, sisters, brothers, and fathers. Of fiancés and best friends. Strangers praying for salvation as they choke in smoky hallways, stumble down bottomless stairwells, and cringe in tiled restrooms, clinging to one another, hoping for hope, praying for fortitude as they succumb to grim resignation.

The fire truck speeds off.

It is 10:16:30. They are eight blocks, give or take, from Ground Zero.[9]

10:17 a.m. to 10:25 a.m.

Tribeca. On every block, I see someone strike up a brief conversation with a person who happens to be nearby. Strangers to one another, likely, who connect as they make their way home on foot. Their features grim. Their eyes cast to the pavement. Their shoulders high and hunched. Their hands balled.

From here, much of the North Tower is visible, but the burn zone is so high I have to lean back and tilt my head until it is perpendicular to my spine to see it. The ash cloud from the remains of the South Tower girdles the massive mound of rubble at the base of its twin.

I need a bathroom, a phone, and water.

Across the street, a man and woman are unlocking the outer door of a warehouse. I call out, "Can you help me?"

They wave me over. At the entrance to the warehouse, they introduce themselves. Paul and Patty.

Inside the door, two German Shepherd dogs growl, snap, and bare their teeth.

A census of dogs in New York City puts the number at 600,000, a guess that includes every iteration of canine, from rhinestone-collared toy poodles in designer handbags to feral mixed breeds roaming alleys. For hours, sirens have been wailing in their sensitive ears and smoke has swept into their snouts. They are beyond unhappy.

"Don't mind the dogs," Paul says. "They won't bite."

They bite.

The warehouse is dark and cavernous. Patty shows me to a small office and points to a multi-line telephone. The dogs curl tight, wary circles around my legs. As soon as she leaves, one sinks his teeth into my ankle. I kick at it, and both dogs slink into the hall. A trickle of blood seeps from the wound. Pfft. It's nothing.

I dictate a quick update to the newsroom and use the bathroom. At the door, Patty hands me a cold bottle of water. Condensation drips down my arm. Bless her heart.

I tell them how grateful I am. Quickly, we exchange contact information. Outside, the air is ashy. I head south toward Ground Zero. After a short way, I glance over my shoulder. Paul and Patty are standing in the doorway, watching me, shaking their heads.

Surely the worst is over.

Just blocks from the flashing lights and mountain of burning rubble at Ground Zero, I stop to look up at the burn zone. Something is falling. No, tumbling. I lose sight of it behind a lower building.

A skinny guy sidles up to me and leans close. "Jumper," he says. His breath smells of coffee. Funny, the things you notice.

I shiver with the realization that what I saw was a man or woman in self-propelled, self-fulfilled, self-sacrificed flight.

"There," the guy says again, his voice at the tattered edge of giddy. "See? Another one."

I throw the jerk a dagger look, and he moves off.

It is an extraordinary sight, a person taking to the sky, a man or woman unmoored from Earth, untethered to anything fixed, weightless, arms transformed into would-be wings as he sails down and down and down, propelled by the invisible pull of gravity to the end of days. I jot the phrases in a notebook.

That's the poetic version. The reality is different.

The sound, for instance. I expect it to be a squishy thud, like the sound of a sack of soil tossed from a truck. It is not. The desperate men and women at the windows, those either jumping or being pushed, travel at terrific speeds and land with dreadful force. The impact sounds like what you would hear when a train plummets off a trestle and crashes to a canyon floor.

I feel swoony. I close my eyes and see myself tumbling, too. The sound plays in my head, haunting, heartbreaking. I tell myself that if I never speak of it, never write about it, I will forget it. Maybe.

It's a false hope, of course. Why don't I see that? For weeks last Spring, I shoved aside the corrosive effect of my abrupt departure from Thornhill. All during the early summer I refused to recognize that I was dangerously depressed. I assumed that if I didn't acknowledge something terrible, it would simply vanish, an assumption that hardly served me well. And yet this day, this moment, and far into the future, I refuse to realize how flawed that mental game is.

10:28 a.m.

The North Tower is three blocks ahead. Or four. I'm not sure.

I pause to rummage in my tote bag for a fresh notebook before continuing on toward the massive jumble of rescue vehicles. It does not occur to me to turn around.

Suddenly, the unthinkable happens.

The entire mass of the North Tower of the World Trade Center begins to sink into itself. Upper floors pancake onto lower ones, as if the magnificent monument to global commerce—levels upon levels of exquisite architecture engineered to support still higher floors—has suddenly liquefied. With savage speed, the skyscraper simply vanishes, along with each body and soul in it. One instant it's there, the next it's a mountain of smoldering rubble pierced with shards.

Dust boils into the autumn air. A ferocious windstorm rockets up the avenues, hundreds of feet high and so thick that whatever is behind it is not visible. Ash and smoke and chunks of God knows what roil across Lower Manhattan. Compressed within the parallel escarpments of lower buildings, the concussive blast travels at jet speed.

Slack-jawed, I stand rooted to the middle of a north-south avenue. With eerie dispassion, I watch death roar toward me. My eyes are sprung. My lungs freeze. My heart races. In the disconnect, I partition time into its fractional components, convinced that every eye blink, every new breath and heartbeat reduces the number of those that remain to me.

Then—and I am talking about slices of seconds here—a frisson of terror races through me. If the North Tower has separated at the burn zone and the top floors are in free-fall, then behind the monumental ash cloud is the whole top of a skyscraper, and it could be toppling this way. Toward me.

Frozen in time and space, I begin a series of bizarre call-and-response calculations.

How many stories tall is the tower?
I don't know.
Guess!
Okay, 175.
Wrong. It was 110 stories tall. So how high is the tower?
I have no idea.
Multiply!
I can't. Not now.
It was 1,730 feet tall, including the antenna. What floors are the burn zone?
I don't know!
How many blocks are you from Ground Zero?
I don't know! A few!
How many feet long are the avenues in Lower Manhattan?
I don't know!
Do the math, Catherine. If you want to know whether the last sight you see is a skyscraper rushing toward you as it barrels to ground, do the math.

I look for a place of safety. Terrified men and women have jammed every recessed doorway, standing with their backs to the street.

Death is careening up the street. In a second, two, the implosion will slam me against a car, a wall, a light pole, and I will die. And the others? The people filling every shallow doorway up and down the street? They will die, too, sucked into the maelstrom, unable to see, to breathe, to find their footing or even perceive whether they are right-side-up or upside down within the hellish blast wave.

If the tower falls this way, it will spare no one.

I duck behind a blue mail bin bolted to the sidewalk and wrap my arms around its metal legs. The roiling thunderhead freight train cyclone dust storm sweeps over and around me. I chuff air thick with ash. Any moment now, I fear I will be crushed. I am certain that I have arrived at the instant of my death. I close my eyes and mourn my children's grieving.

Bits of grit crackle as they strike the mail bin. I hang on tighter and curl up, head between knees. My clothes flap. The howling wind catches at my satchel. In it are my pens and notebooks. I lean out to grab the bag and the world goes dark, silent, and blank.

Having seen bricks and mortar vanish in an instant, having seen men and women on fire soar into thin air on wings of tweed and cotton, having been bitten by a warehouse dog and gifted with water by a stranger, I part from the boundaries of space and the calibrations of time and repair to a more elegiac place.

The windstorm passes.

I get to my feet, brush off dust, and palm back my hair. Later, I will notice that I since right before the North Tower's collapse, I have not made an entry in my notebooks.

No one is running, not anymore. Men and women making their way out of Lower Manhattan on foot are shambling. Yellow-gray dust frosts them head to toe.

I think about the firefighters I spoke with earlier. I check my notebook to see how much time passed between when I last saw their truck pull away from the corner and when the North Tower fell. Just under twelve minutes. Time enough, I know. Time enough to reach Ground Zero before the tower thundered down, carrying every individual in and around it to Earth and raising them, as one, to the heavens.

An F-15 fighter jet whistles across the sky.

Can't look up. Looking up is not good. Dreadful things fall from high places.

I scribble phrases and connect them into sentences.

> I looked up and saw a skyscraper impaled.
> I looked up and saw a tower disappear into its own rubble.
> I looked up and saw human beings leap into thousand-foot voids.
> I looked up and saw another.

Later, I'll try to explain that better, provide context to the enormity of what is happening. But for now, I have no desire to look up at fighter jets, or at anything, and I take great care to avoid doing so.

I walk north, away from the catastrophe at Ground Zero. That decision might not be in the best traditions of fine journalism, but I know I cannot be of use in the burning, billowing maelstrom at the collapse site. Besides, who knows if more buildings are about to thunder down, if more attack planes are on their way, if bombs on the ground are set to go off? No one knows.

I have come within one mailbox of a severe injury this day. I have come close to a violent death. My respect for war correspondents who live with danger was significant before; now, it knows no bounds.

But my sudden, temporary membership among their ranks does.

Shopkeepers and apartment supers are setting televisions on chairs and small tables on sidewalks. They run extension cords through the front doors or open windows. Teens turn up the volume on boom boxes and set them on the stoops. People gather in clots, listening in stunned silence to the latest bulletins. I lean against a limousine and take notes. The car is empty, abandoned on the diagonal in the street, its windows down, its radio blaring the latest news. The keys are in the ignition.

After a while, I head north to TriBeCa and west toward the Hudson River.

Laughter. At the corner of Desbrosses and West streets, laughter bubbles through the open door of the Café F.illi Ponte and rings across the dust and despair of a city brought to its knees. It's jarring, like the soundtrack of a sitcom broadcast at a funeral.

The lunch crowd has arrived early. I guess the F.illi Ponte is as good a place as any to get off the streets, and better than most. A broad bank of windows overlooking the Hudson River draws daylight into a restaurant with exposed brick walls, thick wood ceiling beams, and Italianesque archways.

Customers fill every table. Behind the bar, men in long white aprons scramble to fill glasses of beer and cabernet. Waiters burst from the kitchen with plates of caprese salad and pasta marinara. Silverware clatters over the din of nervous conversation.

There! The laughter again. I turn to see four guys at a window table enjoying a joke. I note their expensive business suits, statement wristwatches, and the fact that there's not a speck of dust on them. I would like to know what's so funny, so I walk over and ask.

One of the guys points to his friend across the table.

"Well," he says, smiling, "that lug has now walked away from two bombings." The lug across the table nods and picks up the thread.

"I was in one of the towers back in '93 when the basement blew up," he says, his voice rising like a stand-up comic delivering a punch line. His colleagues are duly re-amused.

I ask their names. The men spell them for me. I ask the name of their company and they give it. High finance. With that, I am done with them.

I ask the host if I can use an office phone. She waves a hand toward a back hallway. While dictating notes to the Wisconsin newsroom, I notice a shift in the dining room noise. Conversations have stopped in mid-sentence. Chair legs are scraping the floor. Silverware is clinking onto tabletops. I get up and look down the hall. Everyone is rushing for the door.

By the time I hang up, the place is empty. The last two kitchen helpers race past me toward the rear of the restaurant. One of them calls for me to follow.

"Gas attack!" he shouts.

In a dozen long strides, we are in a cool storage area, running past crates of lettuce and tomatoes, cartons of pasta, and shelves stacked with clean towels and cloth napkins.

Have I survived the felling of a skyscraper only to have the simple, essential act of taking a breath fill my lungs with lethal gas? Wouldn't *that* be ironic?

The busboys push through a metal outer door and run down the alley. I squint into daylight and rush head-long out the door after them. The cement landing is surprisingly small, about the size of a card table. It's elevated three feet above the alley so delivery trucks can back up and slide supplies directly into the building. I career off the stoop, land hard in the alley, and drop to my knees, adding scrapes and bruises to my inconsequential miseries.

Pillows of dust rime the tops of parking meters, reminding me of snow in Wisconsin. Each step I take leaves a footprint in the soot. It covers every inch of every car—the hoods, the fenders, side mirrors, everything. A fine film covers my clothes again. I open a notebook to write about it. Within moments, the page is dusty. The pen is dusty. The dust is scalp-deep in my hair. It's in my nose, in my lungs.

What the hell am I breathing?

I see a police officer up ahead. He's got a face mask. Lucky him, I think. He takes it off and hands it to me. As I said, it's that kind of day.

My eyes are gritty. My mouth is gummy and dry. I swallow in spasms. When a sharp cramp tears at my ribs, I slow. Slowing is bad but stopping is worse. Stopping gives me time to think, and this is no day to stop and think.

But I do.

It occurs to me that I have been walking on bodies reduced to powder, leaving footprints on sidewalks that are a communal grave. I am breathing the vaporized remains of human beings and, in so doing, they—the lost souls in the towers, on the planes, on a red fire truck with a hose coiled on the side— they are now an organic part of me. I shake my head, trying in vain to clear the dark thoughts.

I tell myself to call Dr. Donna first chance I get.

12:25 p.m.

A police car slaloms down Ninth Avenue and swerves, narrowly missing a youth in the middle of the street. Afterward, a contrail of dust engulfs the boy. He barely notices.

"We're all dying!" he yells.

A passerby shrugs. "He won't last long," she says.

I run my finger along the wiper blade of an abandoned car and collect an ounce of dust in an empty aspirin bottle. A block later, I stop. If the dust contains the vaporized remains of victims—and it does—then is collecting it a tribute or a sacrilege? I don't know, but I keep the bottle.

On a corner somewhere north of the teeming madness at Ground Zero and south of the empty security of the Paramount, a glass door opens and the aroma of Greek diner food curls out into the September day. Omelets with spinach, cherry tomatoes, and feta cheese. Moussaka burgers prepared with spiced ground lamb, eggplant, and cheesy white sauce. Gyros with tzatziki sauce. The place is packed.

Inside, I call over the counter to a man in a chef's apron. "Got a minute for a couple of questions?"

He does not, but his daughter might. Over there. Clearing plates and glasses from a booth.

Before I leave, I glance up at an ancient black and white television clamped to a wall above a warming oven filled with Greek pizzas. On the screen is the image of a bearded man. His face is long and craggy, his rugged features intense. Piercing black eyes under a pristine white turban. It's impossible to hear the news commentor above the clatter and conversations of the diner, but the caption crawling across the bottom of the screen identifies the man as Osama bin Laden, mastermind of the attacks.

I shrug. Never heard of him.

On the street again, I finish entering notes from the diner interviews.

1:10 p.m.

Penn Station is closed. Locked.

Hundreds of commuters stand outside the station, waiting for it to open. It is 81 degrees and sunny. There isn't a bench or shade tree in sight. Other than what the commuters brought along in their rush to get out of Manhattan, there is no access to food, water, or restrooms nearby. Marooned at the approach to a transit station, they stand in uncharted territory and shuffle their weight foot-to-foot, their features blank. The more uncertain their fate becomes, the more they appear to withdraw into themselves.

I sense the first stirrings of desperation here. No one knows how long the station will be locked. Eventually, night will fall. Darkness can be fearsome.

What might come screaming across a blackened sky? What might happen on a night when almost every officer of the law and emergency responder is either dead or at the foot of the island, frantically searching for survivors?

About 4 p.m.

At the Paramount, a guard checks my driver's license. No one gets in except registered guests. He has a list.

In my room, I turn on the shower and stand under the jets, hands plastered against the tiles. Cool water shears off my face, my shoulders, my elbows. I twist the hot water tap and sink to the floor. Steam spirals to the ceiling. It looks like smoke from the pyre at Ground Zero.

Afterward, I try to phone Dennis and then Claire, but the calls don't go through. I call the newsroom, let them know I'm alive. Then I dial Sheila's room at the Paramount.

"I thought you were dead," she says, sobbing. "I thought you and Rick were dead."

Sheila and I make plans to get together as soon as I collect my thoughts for a first-person story to run alongside the news coverage. Within minutes, though, Rick calls. Would I come with Sheila to his room? He wants to show something to us.

"Give me a half-hour," I tell him. "I'm just starting a personal essay."

4:45 p.m.

Rick's door is ajar. We walk in and see he's set his computer on the bed. He is kneeling on the floor in front of it, tapping the keyboard. Sheila and I peer over his shoulder.

"See that?" he says.

We lean in.

"The dot," he says.

I don't see a dot.

He zooms again. He says he wasn't aware of the dot when he took the shot. I see burning towers. I see smoke and the ghastly burn zone. I see blue sky.

"What do you think?" he asks, still enlarging the image.

Sheila edges toward the door. Rick taps the keyboard twice more.

Now I see.

The dot is someone in the last seconds of life. The dot is an individual falling out of this world into the next. The dot is a man so resigned to his fate that he does not thrash or twist, flap his arms in panic or wheel his legs in futility.

The dot is a human being.

As I stare at the image, dark thoughts swirl and eddy.

Rick's photograph shows a single moment in time. It does not show what happened right after the camera clicks, when the man strikes the ground like a pear tossed from a plane. It does not show what went on before, when the man stood at a blown-out window one hundred stories above the streets of New York, facing certain death. Die in the flames of a jet fuel fire, or at the bottom of a stairwell, in choking smoke, or take to the air and hope to fly.

In such a photograph, there is just the single moment. No before. No after. Just a dot visible against a September sky the color of bluebells.

Most of the time, a reporter's notebook and a photographer's camera are effective barriers between us and the stories we cover. When in the throes of tragedy or crisis, the act of taking photographs or writing notes serves to damper what would be a natural human emotion. We are, after all, employees paid to show or describe, not emote. But in some cases, for some of us, that's not possible.

Rick folds down the cover of his computer and snaps it closed.

Without a word, I move away. I'm at the door when he calls over his shoulder, "Can you send some cutlines?"

Back in my room, I slump in a chair for long minutes, then finish the first-person essay for tomorrow's paper.

An hour later, I meet Rick and Sheila in the hotel dining room. It's eerily empty. Most of the hotel staff has gone home.

"I have soup," the young waiter says, "and rolls from last night."

We each order a drink and then another. The waiter brings the soup. Rick's ringing phone cuts through the silence in the dining room. An editor wants him to take sunset photos of the ash plume. And the city desk would like me to go to Brooklyn tonight, to one of the Islamic neighborhoods there, get quotes from people.

"What kind of quotes?" I ask, wary.

Rick relays the message: "They want you to ask what people in Islamic neighborhoods think about the terrorist attacks."

Nope. Not going. Not doing that.

I have never said a hard no to an assignment in my life. Okay, I did once. An editor told me to go to a women's clinic and pretend I was there to get an abortion. Editors have been known to dole out assignments of questionable merit.

And yet, declining an assignment feels wrong to me now. I tell Rick to tell the editor I'll have an update for the late edition. What I don't say is that I have no intention of going to Brooklyn tonight and walking up to people who look like they might be Islamic (*because really, how would I know?*) and asking them what they think about Osama bin Laden, a man I'd never heard of eight hours ago, blowing up the Twin Towers.

We drain the wine glasses. The waiter clears the table.

Rick says a couple of subway lines are starting to open. He asks if I'm coming.

"Go," I tell him. "Shoot the sunset. It'll be a great picture."

Bryant Park is lovely this evening. In a perfect world, models would be gliding like swans in the tents here, staring into a barrage of camera strobes. But the fashionistas have deserted the tents. The park is quiet as a cemetery.

Up the way, 2,500 men and women pack the pews of St. Patrick's Cathedral. Cardinal Edward M. Egan, a priest of fifty-seven years, a bishop of twenty-nine years, a cardinal of seventeen years, a prince of the Roman Catholic Church, is gowned in silk vestments and a scarlet skullcap. His stentorian voice rings through the soaring edifice and out to the sidewalk. When he refers to Ground Zero as "Ground Hero," applause rises and swells.

At each of the great bronze doors, armed officers stand sentinel, shoulder radios crackling, boot soles shuffling on sanctified ground. I make a note of it.

The crowd files out. Behind them, an organist plays an unusual recessional— "The Battle Hymn of the Republic."

The shadows are lengthening. Dusk is settling on dust, layering unease over heartache.

Across the street, the flags ringing Rockefeller Center droop in the still evening air. Meant to be a beacon of global unity, they represent every member country of the United Nations. I jot a line in my notebook, something about the flags wishing themselves halfway down the poles. Spotlights illuminate the golden sculpture of Prometheus, a Greek god of fire. I make a note of that, too.

7:00 p.m.

Most of the wailing sirens have gone silent. I assume crews of would-be rescuers will work through the night at Ground Zero, but many firefighters and paramedics have gone home or returned to their stations, seeking what solace they can. I'm sure that tourists are hunkering in hotels, trying to connect with relatives back home, and punching telephone buttons for nonexistent room service, too terrified to set out on foot for a restaurant meal, which is nowhere to be found. From one end of The City That Never Sleeps to the other, I envision bewildered parents crawling into bed with their bewildered children, promising to keep the lights on all night.

The last of the day's sunlight slices through slender voids between buildings, gilding the upper city in gorgeousness and boring through the smoke, grit, and human misery at the foot of the island.

Another few blocks, and I am back in Times Square, where this eternal day began. I am beyond exhausted and dazed by the flashing, flickering billboards controlled by automatic timers. At Broadway and 46th Street, I stop. It should be impossible to stand in the middle of the street here, stand minute after minute without a single vehicle swerving or horn honking. On a normal day, several hundred thousand people pass through the Great White Way: tourists in Velcro sneakers and fanny packs snap photos of the jumbotrons, wait in line at the hot ticket box, and fork over $12 cash to sidewalk vendors for a "genuine cashmere" pashmina, crowds moving at half the desired speed of those who live or work in the city.

Tonight, though, the fevered Crossroads of the World is eerily silent and all but deserted. I stand long moments here, alone.

Wait. Is that music?

No. It's birds.

The gigantic, kinetic kaleidoscope that is Times Square is so quiet that I hear birds singing their hearts out. I write a few phrases.

A choir of birds
dulcet elegies
for a city in lament

Back at the hotel, I finish my evening update and phone the newsroom. Afterward, I open emails.

Claire – Mom, I got the messages from your office. I was about to call the *Journal Sentinel* to figure out what the hell happened to you. Please be careful Mom. Love, Claire.

Meg – Bad stuff. OH MY GOD, the World Trade Center. For the first time since getting here, I actually wish I were back in America. I've been trying to call all day. Mom, I really wish you weren't in Manhattan right now! I still have a concert to go to for class tonight It's the LAST thing I want to do. I'll try and call around midnight. And good stuff. Pictures from Wales are attached. Luv, Meg

My sister, Pam – Cathy, sorry I missed your call. I had no idea you were in New York City! Good Lord. Talk about being in the middle of the action. It's a sad day, that's for sure. I'm sure you've got unbelievable stories to tell.

My brother, Tom – I've shown your email to everyone in the office today. They were all amazed, as was I.

My brother, Ken – God bless you, girl, you're always where the action is. Good luck and take care.

Dennis – I got word you are okay. I'm also okay. I've talked to Claire, and she is, too. I left a message for Meg. I love you. God bless. Dennis.

My sister-in-law – I emailed your articles to everyone else in the family so they would know you are all right. I really admire your dedication. Certainly, a life-altering experience none of us can share with you.

True. I will never be the same.

At about eleven, I manage to get a call through to Dennis. His team is west of Washington D.C., headed back to Milwaukee by car. He is stunned to hear that I left the hotel to cover the attacks.

"Why did you do that? Why would you put yourself in danger like that?" These are not questions; they're accusations.

"My editor said 'GO.'"

"You just told me you phoned her. You told me you offered."

"I assumed it was just a big fire in a tall building."

"You knew it was a monumental tragedy."

I counter, my voice rising. "Nobody knew the first tower would collapse." *God, I hate that I sound petulant and whiney.*

"After that, you should have known the second tower could come down, too."

Now I'm mad.

"Nobody knew that! And besides, by then I knew this was a huge story. I *wanted* to go."

We end the call, each disappointed in the other. I sit on the bed and draw my knees to my chest, mulling over his words. He is furious because he is hurt and scared. I am furious because I expected him to admire me, not castigate me. I tell myself that Dennis will come around, that in time, when he's given it some thought, surely he'll be proud of me.

In that, I am wrong.

It's midnight. Although I'm bone-tired, my mind keeps returning to the moment the North Tower blasted floury remains by the tonnage into the air, across the land, onto everything on the land. Time and again, I replay the collapse. Each time my thoughts skitter off to earlier times, as if to avoid reliving the horror of a catastrophic day. In frustration, I make a few notes on a pad of hotel paper. While the idea is fresh, I want to get it down. I start with phrases, knit them into sentences, and then into a long, rambling paragraph. I'll fix it later.

Granulated clouds boil up avenues paved over land, land right here where Lenape tribes once camped. Waded salt marshes with spears in hand, probing summertime banks for oysters to roast over open fires.

Bankers and merchants from Holland arrived by sea, fleshy men in waistcoats and breeches and shoes with buckles, men lured by the aroma of money. Soon, they raised a settlement here, right here. They named the place, land they assumed was theirs, New Amsterdam, and quickly, for this was important to them, they erected a fort to defend their lucrative fur trade. Here. Right here.

They brought over their pale wives and children, for the Dutchmen were wealthy and they were lonely, and they assumed now is forever, which it is not, not ever.

In time, the British Royal Navy sailed into view, warships and transports laden with disciplined troops and mighty guns. Shots rang out. Fires raged. Blood spilled. The British fought the Dutch to the death, here, right here, and prevailed.

And stayed, the British, for they, too, made assumptions. Unlike the Lenape but quite like the Dutch, the British figured this land was their land, a fact disproved by General Washington and his remaining troops, who fought on and on after fighting the British to the death at Valley Forge, less than three miles from here.

The general was inaugurated the first president of the United States of America, and took the oath of office at Federal Hall, which is a matter of blocks from the glorious towers with ice-white ribs that invaders burned to flinders this very day. All that, so close that I could walk from there to here. In fact, I did.

So much history under the dust this night. Not dust. Not debris, either. Remnants of what was and is no more. The remains of those who lived and died on a sunny September morning.

I lay down my pen, lost in visions of downtown Manhattan. In my mind, I see a vast cloud swirling from the Battery over open water to a torch held aloft, one that has welcomed armadas of immigrants—craftsmen, clockmakers and cooks, shoemakers and stonemasons, pig farmers and such. Those finally released from quarters below the waterline stood in families, fathers in caps and grandmothers in shawls, boys in knee pants and girls in pinafores. They leaned out over deck railings, cheering even as they wept for joy at the sight of a copper torch and, beyond it, the great, teeming, vertical city of New York, doorway to a land fertile with promise.

I stand at the single window in my room and gaze out, mesmerized. The Paramount is miles from the seething rubble at Ground Zero, and yet beyond the window flecks of grit swirl on currents of night air like dry snowflakes. I watch, unblinking, and record in my heart this moment, as the remains of the day rise and fall by the billions.

Remember, I tell myself.

Remember every bit and piece of September 11, 2001, when the world tilted off true, when time stretched like clocks in a Dali painting, when minutes lingered like silent regret and hours sped by like fires in the sky.

From morning coffee and a sidewalk stroll to midnight melancholy at a hotel window, remember it all.

I look up, finally, to a wedge of night sky. Above a burnt and blistered city, a city in mourning at the edge of a nation bereaved, stars spatter the heavens.

Barricades, Wednesday, September 12, 2001

Chapter 9
Collective Foreboding
September 12 – 15, 2001

Teardrops of light flicker

Wednesday, September 12

I WAKE BEFORE dawn, exhausted, headachy, and vaguely sick to my stomach. I'm tempted to curl up in bed, but I know I won't. I'll go out and report a day-after story. A feature writer is a reporter. A fashion writer is, too. I am the only reporter from the *Milwaukee Journal Sentinel* who's here, so far at least. As I see it, my job is to do what I do best—describe what is happening here, be an eye-witness for readers a thousand miles away. Get up. Go out. Write what I see, hear, and feel so they will better understand what *here* is like.

Sheila and I take a taxi down to Greenwich Village and join a small group of journalists across the street from the emergency entrance of St. Vincent's Hospital. The city is filled with journalists who traveled here for the runway shows, but I have seen only one other fashion writer yesterday and this morning. I don't get it. Where are they?

For a hundred and fifty years, St. Vincent's has been the main medical center in Lower Manhattan. But this morning, doctors and nurses stand silent beside empty gurneys lined up on the sidewalk. They talk in hushed tones as they keep vigil, awaiting an influx of injured patients to treat, repair, save. But there is no surge, not even a trickle, so complete was the loss of life.

Eventually, we walk on.

Farther down, police have cordoned off the streets around Ground Zero. At one of the barricades, I talk with three officers. Later, I fold their words, their hopes and fears, into an article for Thursday morning's paper.

I begin the story with a sweeping description of a city withdrawn in collective foreboding. Banks are dark. Schools, libraries, corporate offices, and corner shops are shuttered. Hair salons, literary agencies, construction companies, vegetable stalls, bakeries, and laundromats are empty, unlit, and locked.

I describe the exhausted, grieving officers of the NYPD I met, the men and women of the FDNY, and their colleagues throughout the Northeast who are working in shifts here—or who never left—grim-faced teams of firefighters and police officers, the detection dogs, and volunteers determined to unearth survivors or bring out the dead. There's a rumor that yesterday they found twenty-one people alive.

"And today?" I ask one of the officers at the barricades. "So far, today?"

She shakes her head.

I ask her what it's like for the rescuers. She tells me they're breathing smoke and ash, stepping over exposed shards, digging furiously with shovels and picks, clawing with bare fingers if they hear the bleep-bleep of a buried cellphone. She says the mountain of ruins is four stories high.

At a barricade on Houston Street, within sight of the ash cloud that plumes over the tip of the island like a shroud, I stop to talk with one of the NYPD officers on duty. He's thirty years old. He started work at ten o'clock yesterday morning, worked until midnight, and was back at four o'clock. Now, at mid-morning, the sun is punishing. Beads of sweat dot his forehead. He's dusty and sleep-deprived and most certainly anxious, but he doesn't complain.

Within hours after the towers fell, the *Journal Sentinel* sent a small team of reporters and photographers to New York by car. Later today, the bridges and tunnels reopen, and the team makes its way to the Paramount. Tonight, we have dinner together at Café Un Deux Trois, a casual Italian place near the hotel. Sheila doesn't join the thread of subdued conversation. She hardly touches the food. Instead, she draws sketches on the paper tablecloth, colorful images of the city skyline as it was the day we arrived. Sheila is a journalist, a newspaper designer but not a news gatherer. She is not here on assignment. She came on her own time, on her own dime, on a lark. The few times she looks up from her meal, I see pools of despair in her soft eyes.

What must she see in my eyes? Could she see the words, phrases, bits of description flowing across my field of vision right now, much like they streak across a computer screen? Would she see my lush descriptions of unfathomable tragedy, my fear and anger, my ambition? Would she see the heartache that is drowning me, the sorrow consuming a fashion writer who lacks the skill to convey the monumentality of it all?

Would she see in my eyes the regret I feel for not writing more, not recording every detail, not describing scenes clearly enough, for failing to find words as fierce and dire as what happened before my eyes?

Would she see I am sinking again, weighted with remorse because I am certain the firefighters I met by the telephone kiosk died minutes after I lost sight of their truck? It is unbearable, the thought that if I had only kept them a bit longer, asked more questions, gone over the spelling of their first and last names, inquired about their children, double-checked and triple-checked, I would have delayed their departure.

I would have saved their lives.

Can Sheila and the others ordering red wine and pasta tonight see in my eyes the profound despair I am doing my best to conceal?

Quickly, I turn my gaze to the menu.

The members of the team agree to meet in the morning and coordinate our assignments. It's an early night. All of us are wasted.

Thursday, September 13, 2001

I assumed the thick, blue-gray smoke boiling over Lower Manhattan would be gone by now. It isn't. I have no idea how long the rubble will fester, but I know it isn't just smoke rising into the air. It's pulverized drywall and glass, crushed computers and blackened carpeting, bathroom sinks and tubes of lipstick. Cinnamon rolls half-baked. Eggs lightly scrambled. And the microscopic remains of 2,763 people in and around the towers, including the doomed passengers and crews on the planes, and the suicidal hijackers.

I had planned to go to Brooklyn today. I got a tip about a famous cemetery there, Green-Wood, 478 rolling acres studded with headstones that mark the final resting place of famous New Yorkers. I heard that on Tuesday morning a cemetery worker stood on a hill and watched the unfolding catastrophe. His wife was at her desk in one of the lower buildings destroyed in the collapse.

The wind has freshened. I heard it is carrying sheafs of paper with singed edges across the East River, and they land on Green-Wood's manicured graves.

It'll make a good story.[10]

I pack a satchel and go down to the lobby. The minute I push through the front doors of the hotel, I stop. My story is right in front of me.

The searchers. The fliers.

In the forty-eight hours since terrorists speared planes into the towers, an army of anguished individuals has been searching the city for what is rarely attainable: a miracle.

Theirs is an unfolding story with universal themes—death-defying love, longing over logic, hope unvanquished, hope enduring, hope that brooks no reason. It's a picture I can paint with words to illustrate this grievous place on this lead-sky September day.

I walk for hours. Everywhere I go, the searchers have been.

Fevered with worry, fueled by steely resolve, the friends and families of the merely missing, the merely lost, gathered in kitchens and living rooms and offices to pore over wedding albums, personnel files, yearbooks, and pictures displayed on mantles and bedside tables. When they found the right image, they pasted it on a sheet of computer paper and wrote below it a name, an age, the floor number of a tower that is no more.

They hunkered over home printers or took their work to a store that makes copies and ran off fliers by the ream. Then they bore their burden into the streets, soldiers on a mission with long odds.

Yesterday, starting before dawn and continuing into nightfall, they affixed fliers with string to lampposts, tacked fliers to fences, taped fliers to walls.

Recorder of Deeds   71

They are out again this morning, the searchers, fanning out across the urban grid, hanging and tacking and taping fliers by the thousands, transforming Manhattan and its sister boroughs into kiosks. By now, fliers dot the facades of office buildings at street level, stick to restaurant windows, cling to scaffolding around construction sites, encircle bus-stop poles. They appear in swanky office lobbies and luxury boutiques, on the doors of antique book shops and plastered to the sides of shoeshine stands. I heard a man say he saw them taped to the inside of a restroom stall door.

The searchers are everywhere, trudging along block after block, banking on the off-chance that a single passerby amid a flowage of millions might recognize a face. With bloodshot eyes they scan the crowds, their features set and grim even as they cling spectacularly to hope.

I pause at a collage comprised of dozens of broadsides, each an unintended paradox that burns in my chest. The dust still swirls in the air, and yet here they are, the victims, smiling for a snapshot taken on some happy occasion in the past.

Do the families think their lost husband or wife, son or daughter has merely wandered off or forgotten to come home? Do they believe that by some sweet alchemy they were somehow spared and thus, somehow, could be found?

They do, the grim parents, spouses, friends. The searchers who pasted a snapshot to a sheet of typing paper, added a name, an age, a floor number of a tower where in another time, in a different world, their loved one drew breath.

I pass pictures by the thousands, photos taken before anyone suspected there would be an after. Grooms in ruffled shirts. Brides in gowns of lace. Dozens of grooms. Dozens upon dozens of brides.

Across the street from the Plaza Hotel, a woman emerges from a limousine and waits for the driver to unload a mountain of designer luggage. I hold my breath as a searcher approaches her, assuming he will be rebuffed. But she accepts a flier from his outstretched hand and in return receives from him a tight smile of thanksgiving.

A smile is an ephemeral thing, though. As I watch, the face of the searcher falls back into fissures of grim resolve.

I suspect that walking fills their empty hours with purpose. I suspect it keeps denial alive. I suspect this is why, against all odds, they forge on.

At 72nd and Central Park West, I approach a montage on the front of the famous Dakota Apartment building. Sandy is missing; he has multiple tattoos. Please call this number if you see Sandy. Augustine is a firefighter with a wife and three kids. Tonyell's gold necklace sets off her pretty face. Andrew was last seen wearing a green Izod shirt. Laurence's blood type is AB negative. Rosemarie is a mother of six.

Another block, another hundred grooms and brides, graduates holding diplomas and mothers holding infants.

The day is cool and drizzly under a low shelf of clouds. I walk past a firehouse where well-wishers have left flowers and small mementos. The weather has soaked mounds of stuffed bunnies and teddy bears. The bouquets are bedraggled. Hand-printed words drizzle in runnels down notes of sympathy.

Back in Times Square, street vendors are doing a booming business in FDNY tee shirts, twin towers keychains, and $1.79 Statues of Liberty. Just like that, while paying for a cheap poncho, my mind replays the moments I crouched behind the mail bin. Lost in memory, I don't notice the line has moved forward. The woman behind me taps my shoulder. I gasp and jump to the side, as startled as if she had swatted me with a stick.

Raindrops spatter the side of vendor's cart. The fliers taped to it are damp. At the slightest breeze, two of them shear off and take to the air.

For now, I feel a strange commonality with the searchers, suspended in the pitiful interlude before reality extinguishes the foundless, boundless hope of the human heart.

Holding back tears, I stand in the rain and write.

Friday, September 14, 2001

I keep hearing sirens. I keep hearing play-yard sand sifted through a colander and trains falling to canyon floors. Each time the phone rings or a door shuts, I jump a mile.

Tomorrow morning, I'll try to get back to Milwaukee and call Dr. Donna. Tonight, I have one last story to do.

New Yorkers are planning candlelight vigils in remembrance of the victims. One of the largest gatherings will take place in Union Square Park in the Flatiron neighborhood. It's the closest public space to Ground Zero.

Rick, Sheila, and I get there early. I've already looked up the background of the park and stored it in my laptop computer.

Union Square Park opened in 1839 on land that had been a cemetery for the poor. In the 1870s, Frederick Law Olmsted and Calvert Vaux redesigned the grounds, taking care to leave a good measure of open space so people would gather there. Over the years, statues of Washington, Lincoln, Gandhi, and Lafayette have presided over rallies, protests, festivals, and Sunday strolls.

By early afternoon, mourners fill the interior of the park. Many had first stopped on the sidewalk to stare at the fliers covering a twelve-foot-high Wall of the Missing.

Blustery wind and a steady drizzle add to the miseries of the day. It doesn't seem to matter to the people at the vigil. Some carry bouquets tied with thin, floppy ribbons. Others write poems or sentiments of sorrow on the huge sheets of paper volunteers set out for them. Someone drapes an American flag over the statue of George Washington.

A woman next to me says, "You know, the last time this city was attacked was in 1776."

I know.

Through the afternoon, the crowd builds. Parents brought babies bundled against the chill. Boys brought dogs on leashes and girls brought flags on sticks. Seniors carried fliers encased in plastic. Organizers came with colored chalk, packets of Kleenex, candles and matches.

Each of them, all of them, arrived with fading hope and abiding sorrow.

By dusk, under a chilly, stubborn rain, a crowd of thousands stands shoulder to shoulder, filling the park grounds and spilling out onto nearby streets. Some people weep without embarrassment. Others sing hymns and patriotic anthems.

At nightfall, clouds obscure the moon and stars, but the rain lets up. Organizers squat to empty water from glass votives. Those in the crowd withdraw candles from handbags and coat pockets, backpacks, and plastic sacks.

I hear the elongated *schht* of a match tip drawn across the abrasive strip of the packet. Then another. Soon, dozens and dozens of people are lighting matches or rolling the metal spark wheels of cigarette lighters. In the gathering gloom of a dark and desperate time in America, in a park studded with statues of patriots long dead, teardrops of light flicker in the night, illuminating the faces of the living in circlets of grief.

Saturday, September 15, 2001

Sheila is gone. Checked out of the hotel. I don't know when or how. I know she was worried about getting a seat on a plane, and she was certainly under no obligation to stay. My guess is that either late last night, after the vigil, or early this morning she got on a westbound train.

She must have been in a hurry; she didn't stop at the door to my room to say goodbye.

Rick and I have tickets for a flight leaving around noon from Philadelphia. We tip the Paramount doorman handsomely to whistle down a taxi and convince the driver to take us to Philly. The price of the ride is $300. We don't blink.

I slide into the back seat and set up my computer on my lap. On the drive to Philadelphia, I finish my story about the vigil. I have just enough time to call the newsroom in Milwaukee and dictate the story to a friend on rewrite before we get to the airport. Over the highway noise, I hear her crying.

Chapter 10
Homecoming
Sunday, September 15, 2001

So much more to tell

DENNIS IS RATTLING around the kitchen. Opening the fridge, slapping a sack of bread on the counter. Then lunch meat, sliced cheese, a jar of mustard.

Will it never end?

"Want a sandwich?"

It must be noon. I'm still in my nightgown and robe.

Yesterday, breakfast was a cup of coffee at the Paramount Hotel. Lunch was an airport sandwich in Philadelphia. Dinner was carry-out pizza at home in Whitefish Bay, which I choked down so Dennis would see that I am eating. During the night, dreams of the debris cloud fountaining down were so vivid, so real, that I woke trembling. Early this morning, I managed to transfer myself from our bed to the family room sofa. I haven't moved since. I keep slipping out of time and place. The anguished streets of Lower Manhattan seem more vivid and familiar to me than my own home. I keep dozing, keep startling each time Dennis closes a cabinet door or drops a fork. Our doorbell is a two-note chime that today wails like a fire truck siren. Ghastly images swirl in my head. "Um, sandwich? Not yet."

He gives me a look. "When then? It's almost two."

I don't care. I don't want food. You see, honey, I have a problem. The gun is back. The gun the gun the beautiful silvery gun is back. I know I should make it go away, but the thing is, I want it to stay.

Dennis goes upstairs to get a pillow for me. As soon as he's out of sight, tears well up and stream down my cheeks. Before he returns, I wipe my face with the cuff of my bathrobe. I don't want him to see me cry. He's still sullen because I left the safety of the hotel; I don't want to give him a fresh reason to be irked. Dennis tries to hide his worry, which is helpful. He is loving and attentive, but also judgmental and deeply resentful, which is not helpful.

As he sees it, I risked my life needlessly, risked daughters losing their mother, risked a husband losing his wife, and thought nothing of the pain it would cause them, all for a newspaper story that droves of other journalists were reporting.

I see it differently.

I did not intend to put myself in grave danger. I did not walk out of the Paramount Hotel on the morning of 9/11 thinking, "Well, if I get killed on the job today, so be it." I love my job, but not enough to die for it.

The fact is, I am proud of what I did. What I regret is not being braver, not getting the stories I would have gotten if I had gotten even closer to the towers. I will always regret the brevity of my interviews with those firefighters, for a longer list of questions and answers would have delayed them, possibly enough to save them.

Finally, I regret not writing more. There was so much more to tell.

Throughout the afternoon, Dennis tries to engage me in conversation about household issues, about Claire and Meg, about our cat. I try to respond, but my focus skitters right back to New York. Frankly, I do not see the point of chatting about the weather when human life is so fragile, so finite, when on any given day, at any instant, a 110-story skyscraper could come crashing down, and the clock that marks our time on Earth would stop.

I realize he is using easy conversation to try to pull me back to here and now. He knows I have been through a terrifying ordeal. He can see I am drained. What he can't see is how quickly and profoundly I'm falling into an abyss again.

the gun the gun the gun the gun the gun the

He is trying his best to anchor me to our home and to our lives here, but I am adrift. Our stuttering attempts at conversation give way to silence, and I nod off again. Dennis tucks the phone number of Dr. Donna in the pocket of my robe, pulls a pan of soup off the stove, and keeps watch.

I sleep deeply and dream about a crenelated skyline drizzling down into water, sizzling as it disappears beneath the surface.

When I wake, it's dark. I dial the phone with effort. My right hand aches. The hand that held a pen and filled notebooks. The hand that wrote words to describe the sound a body makes when it falls from the heights and lands on the roof of a lower building. The hand that took down a firefighter's words as he gripped a telephone receiver and said goodbye to Mikey. The hand that wrote the words a prince of the church said to his flock as he tried to assure them that a better world awaits those who were lost.

As I slept, I must have contracted my right hand into a tight fist. I've been doing that all week. Releasing the tension feels unnatural. I have no idea why, but when I wrap my fingers around my thumb and clench again, it feels right.

On Sunday night, I lever myself off the sofa. On Monday morning, I take a shower. On Tuesday I go back to work.

After the initial flurry of greetings, I occupy myself in the least taxing way possible: I open the press releases that accumulated while I was gone. An assistant editor approaches. Would I do a story about how modern women are hanging their laundry on clotheslines?

Have you lost your mind? I have just covered the story of the century and you want me to write about laundry?

Silence hangs heavy between us. Finally, she walks away. She looks as thoroughly annoyed as I am. Much later, I realize she had not come to me with a petty assignment; her story idea was the thoughtful gesture of a woman who simply wanted to help ease me back into the job.

Other staffers are not so generous.

One of the elite bureau reporters for our paper has flown back to Milwaukee for some much-needed face-time in the newsroom. The logistics of 9/11 left her out of the paper's main coverage. Eventually, she wanders to the Features Department and plants a hip on my desk.

"How you doing?" she asks, leafing through my copy of *Vogue*.

It's not an actual question. She has no interest in how I am doing. We have never spoken to one another.

Before I muster an answer, she drops the magazine, picks up a photograph of my daughters, and runs her thumb across the top of the frame. I have been out of the office more than a week. I have been back at my desk ten minutes. And a newsroom isn't a surgicenter. Dust slides off the frame and flurries into the air. Zing! I am straight back in New York, rushing from the Café F.illi Ponte and leaving footprints in the dust of the towers.

The important reporter from the important bureau examines her thumb with exaggerated distaste, blows off motes of dust, lifts her haunch from my desk, and departs without a word.

Good reporters are competitive. A display of dominance by an A-list reporter who was on the sidelines of a monumental story is expected. And good editors are inquisitive, so in the days to come, what surprises me is that not a single editor has beckoned me to a quiet office for a debriefing. Or asked me if there is anything I didn't have the time, space, or clarity of thought to write about from New York. No one asked me to do a follow-up piece, an essay or package of short items wrapped around a central theme. No one said, "Have you anything more to tell our readers?"

Lots! Tons! The sounds. The smells. Dried blood on my ankle. Empty baby strollers in the street. Men and women in the air, arms outstretched, as if in exigency human arms could become wings.

The sound when they landed.

The fear in the eyes of the firefighters waiting to make a brief, agonizing call home. Their fingers trembling as they dialed.

More, oh more.

Why don't I offer?

Why don't they ask?

The book editor wraps me in a bear hug, says I look thinner, asks if I lost weight. Colleagues stop at my desk on their way to the cafeteria for coffee. They pause to ask how I'm doing. A quick "okay" seems to be what they expect, so that's what I say and they move on. Before, I would have joined them. They mean well. But I've changed in ways too fundamental and profound for me to even acknowledge, much less examine. I am different now, and I cannot bring myself to chat on the way to coffee about the current state of how the hell I'm doing. Once started, I might never stop.

I'm not so good. I startle at the sound of a kitchen cabinet closing or a soda can opening. I sleep too much, and I want to sleep even more.

I can't look up.

I'd like to talk to you about the terror that sizzled through me when I didn't know which way the North Tower was falling. I'd like to show you the blank pages in my notebook when the world tilted 10 degrees off true. I'd like you to know the depth of the bewilderment I'm hiding this very minute. I'd like you to know I'm drowning in sadness.

Later, my friend Michele proposes we go out to lunch. We stroll the Milwaukee River pedestrian walkway toward a downtown mall with a food court. On the way, I glance at the sky. Big mistake. The puffy cumulus clouds are identical to the plume above Ground Zero, and for the next couple of minutes I am not headed for a mall with a food court. I am back in Lower Manhattan. I am on the West Side Highway. I am staring slack-jawed at the void where the South Tower used to be.

Workers have built scaffolding over the Milwaukee sidewalk. I don't want to walk under scaffolding. I don't want to be underneath anything. Things fall. Falling things kill people.

I panic and stop. Soon, Michele is well ahead. I hear above me the footfalls of construction workers on wood planking. Suddenly, sparks from a welder's tool shower down onto the sidewalk near me. For a moment, I freeze in place. Then I run.

By the time I catch up to my friend, I can hardly breathe.

The *Journal Sentinel* is posting highlights of its 9/11 coverage on its web site. The digital content editor has put up some of Rick's fabulous photos along with a terrific story by a woman on the team who spent a grim night at one of the hard-hit Manhattan firehouses.

A colleague in Features notices that the paper has not posted my stories. I walk across the newsroom and confront the digital content manager. He appears surprised. He says he'll call it to the attention of a higher editor. On the way back to my desk, I wonder why he hasn't posted my work, and why he needs permission from someone else to do so. The following day, my dispatches appear on the site.

Next, I learn that community organizations have phoned the newsroom requesting 9/11 speakers for their upcoming meetings, and that someone has told the clerk who answers the calls to transfer them to Rick. Why didn't he tell me? This prompts me to take another walk across the newsroom.

What I really want to do, though, is lay on the sofa, clench my fist, and sleep.

For the last three months, a neurologist has worked to minimize my migraine headaches, a psychiatrist has worked to keep my phantom gun at bay, a massage therapist has worked to knead knots of tension out of my shoulders, and I have worked to rebuild my relationship with my father. All while under pressure to report, research, and write newspaper articles on deadline.

Back in late August, when it was time to firm up travel plans and contact designers for tickets to their upcoming Fashion Week shows, I believed I had conquered what ailed me. The fog of hopelessness had lifted. The visions had faded. I was alert and focused. On the few occasions my mind wandered, it took me back to a time well before 9/11, took me back to Wabi.

Chapter 11
Connections
1960s and 1970s

Life was grand

I'M GOING TO Wabi!

In early June of 1963, Pam and I fill matching steamer trunks with blue and white shorts, tee shirts, and sweatshirts embroidered with CW, Camp Wabigoniss. It is the first of three large gifts our grandfather gave us over the years. Thanks to A.J., we spent two months at an elite equestrian camp in northern Wisconsin. I slept in a log cabin built before my parents were born. I posted to the trot on thoroughbred horses tacked with English saddles, raced vintage wood canoes across a pristine lake, and braided lanyards destined for little use. I learned to execute low forehand shots on clipped-grass tennis courts that befuddled the camper on the other side of the net, the daughter of a governor. It was the most idyllic summer of my life.[11]

Chapter 12
Harvest
Late September 2001

Squares on a magical chess board

ONE SATURDAY AFTERNOON, Dennis takes me on a long, meandering country drive. Fresh air, he says, is medicinal. I cut him one of those marital looks.

You've got to be kidding me.

But it's 65 degrees and sunny and the trees are starting to turn color, so off we go. Dennis takes city streets and then county roads out to Milwaukee's scenic northern exurbs. We roll down the windows and for an hour or more I am at peace.

Wisconsin Septembers are nothing like Missouri's.

In St. Louis, early autumn feels like summer, and summer feels like the interior of a furnace. By the first of June, heat-thickened air smears across the Great Plains and settles over Missouri for a stupefying, four-month encampment. Day after day, St. Louisans vilify in Promethean terms the substance they struggle to inhale. I once heard a wheezy woman say she felt as if she was sucking air through a gol-durn horse blanket.

Shortly after sunup, heat narcotizes the wakening city. Morning temperatures lumber up to triple digits of Fahrenheit. Throughout the urban grid, atmosphere more viscous than gaseous undulates in waves over streets baking to a crisp. Accountants in sweltering offices loosen neckties. Stenographers pluck at their skirts, perspiring in places too unmentionable to itemize. Babies chafe and fuss. Grandmothers make pitchers of sweet tea.

From the Mississippi River westward, chigger-bitten children dispensed from purgatorial schoolrooms with a final clanging bell and a year-end report card hurry home to seek relief in the gushings of open hydrants, under the spitting jets of garden sprinklers, in shady country club basins or tepid community pools. Farther out, strands of haze curl through creek-threaded valleys.

By late afternoon, choruses of lovestruck cicadas rouse themselves to tympanic song, and the verges throb with longing. Fireflies bejewel back yards with conversations broadcast in diamond-like code. At nightfall, the heat ignites pyrotechnic shows in pillowed clouds which whole families watch from patios and kitchen windows, gaping at electric flickers along the horizon, ominous but harmless, usually.

In empurpled darkness, the last, dawdling breeze stills, and the few St. Louisans who still lack air conditioning embark on Quixotic quests for ventilation. When I was a child, nobody I knew had central air. Everybody had fans, instead, oscillating throughout summer and early fall on sills, pivoting in repetitive futility. Chiffon curtains billowed and collapsed.

We lived in Chafford Woods back then, in a small brick Cape Cod with a red front door. In the evening, I could see the neighbors' televisions and bedside lamps beyond their screen windows, glowing in alternating shades of silver and gold. I'd pretend the windows were squares on a magical chessboard. If shadows glided across the openings, I thought up stories about them. One silhouette would be a gossamer queen caped in velvet and leading a procession along a gilded hall. Another, a young prince ruffled at the neck racing cousins of noble birth through a boxwood maze. Called to bed, I would drift off to moonstruck visions of knights gallant clad in sterling exoskeletons that sparked with starlight. In my dreams, the valiants held heraldic flags, long triangles of satin that fluttered in the breeze. With the grace of ballet dancers and the surety of warriors, they mounted great white stallions, eager, side-prancing animals so fleet that as they took to the gallop their hooves spun above the cobblestones and their tails streamed like silken threads. Drowsy, I watched my knights until they pierced distant forests of my own creation and vanished into stands of shivering aspen.

In short, early autumn in St. Louis was and still is hot.

But September in Wisconsin is gorgeous. Driving through gently rolling countryside, Dennis and I pass third-generation farmhouses and octagonal barns that preside over fields pebbled with pumpkins. Tractors churn in the distance. Pastured cows graze the last green tufts. Later, shaggy horses will stand at fences, streaming white vapor into the chilly air. Frost will girdle ponds. Shallow streams will ice over, and beneath the thin, chalky surface, water clear as glass will course rocky beds.

It is high school football season. Our house is three blocks from Whitefish Bay High School. The cheers and groans of the fans carry the pathos of home games well beyond the spectator stands. On Friday nights, marching bands take to the field, and the bright sound of trumpets is part of the charm of Whitefish Bay.

By the middle of October, I am more productive and engaged at work. Whether that is due to easy assignments, therapy sessions, anti-anxiety medication, or simply that a month has passed since 9/11, I cannot say.

By the time trucks mounded with balsam pines and Frazier firs rumble onto Christmas tree lots, I hope to feel stirrings of holiday cheer.

At the end of the year, I am gratified to be nominated for *Milwaukee Journal Sentinel* Writer of the Year. Lush letters of nomination submitted by editors and by my peers cite the Death Row story, the Fashion Week coverage, and my 9/11 dispatches. When I read one nomination that predicts I will forever carry the week of 9/11 in my heart, I am surprised someone actually understands.

> Catherine – Daughters, I'm a happy woman this afternoon. I just found out my story about the prison minister won first place in the Features category of the Wisconsin Newspaper Assn competition.
>
> Claire – Woo hoo, Mom! Didja win any money! Are ya going to be famous with your picture in the paper? Oh wait, you already have your picture in the paper.

It takes a world-changing, wife-shattering event to wrest Dennis from the enveloping familiarity of Whitefish Bay, where he was born and schooled, where his childhood home stood but a block or two from ours, now.

He knows every alley and avenue, every house. He would live in The Bay forever.

My later childhood was in Thornhill Estates, a private, gated neighborhood of homes built in the 1960s and 1970s. In The Bay, property is measured by the linear foot, garage doors open to alleys, fences and hedges define the boundaries of those who live in close quarters. The lots of Thornhill Estates are platted by the acre. Driveways are long and wide. Expansive lawns meld visually with one another. Dogs and kids roam unfettered.

I loved it there.

But the differences are even more profound. Every family in Thornhill Estates came from somewhere else. Everyone arrived as a newcomer, eager to make fresh connections and friendships.

In Whitefish Bay, many residents remain from cradle to grave, departing only temporarily and only to top off a Whitefish Bay education with a degree from the University of Wisconsin, eighty-four miles down the road. Social circles set generations earlier hold fast down through the years. In many cases, children and their parents live a block or two from grandparents. If that is your family, it's wonderful. But if Whitefish Bay is four hundred miles from your family home, it can be challenging, especially during holidays.

When planners laid out the residential lots of The Bay, they set the houses so close to one another that the chatter of a television show, the clatter of dinner dishes, even casual or intimate conversations in a bedroom with an open window transmit to the next-door neighbors with crystal clarity.

For years, decades, I have yearned for a newer house with long views, a house like Thornhill. In the fall of 2001, I get my wish. Frankly, had I wished for a tropical island with monkeys, Dennis would have made it happen.

On one of our weekend drives, he and I discover a subdivision in its early stage of development. The first homes in it are large and beautiful. Substantial areas will remain in their natural state, with marshes and ponds, wetlands, and wildlife. We tour a model and talk with the developer.

In early November of 2001, construction begins on the 3,200-square-foot house of my dreams. Our lot in Hidden Reserve is at the end of a cul de sac. The front windows will look down a lane flanked on one side by slender trees. The back will have views across a deep lawn, a row of low bushes, and on to a country club fairway.

Our great room will have a vaulted ceiling, custom wood cabinetry, a fireplace, and a wet bar. The kitchen will be enormous, with granite counter tops, double Wolf ovens, and a Sub-Zero fridge. French doors will lead to a brick patio I designed to mimic Thornhill's. For Dennis, there will be a room we call the Cornelius Vanderbilt study. By next October, Hidden Reserve will be ready for us.

It will be my refuge, my safe place.

Chapter 13
Normal
2002

Alive and kicking

THROUGHOUT THE WINTER and early spring, I am happy choosing tile and marble for bathrooms, granite for kitchen countertops, even doorknobs and hinges for the new house. Dennis and I drive up to the outskirts of Sheboygan and tour the Kohler showroom. I fall in love with a sink painted with woodlands and game birds. It would be nice to have Claire and Meg here for second opinions. Sometimes I am overswept with yearning for them.

During my darkest hours, they shine bright.

> Catherine – Hi there, dearies. Your loving mother hasn't heard from either of you in 48 hours, wondering if you're still alive.

> Meg – What, so I'm supposed to contact you every 48 hours?

> Claire – yes mother. Still alive and kicking. Well, alive at any rate. How's mom?

> Claire is in Chicago, working, acting in indie theater productions, and sampling relationships with boyfriends we hope will someday be someone else's son-in-law.

> Claire – I'm not doing too good today, Mom. You-Know-Who picked a fight with me, called me names, ripped on my theatre company, said he hates the world and everyone in it, asked me to leave his apartment, then changed his mind, then sent me an email saying he was unhappy with our relationship. Do I know how to pick 'em, or what?

> Claire – I finally got my cat. I have to give her antibiotics, though. I might try and give her a bath, too.

Claire – Hi mom! Just wanted to say hello and thank you for a lovely weekend and thank Dad for filling up my car with gas.

Claire – I just told someone at work that this weather is Kafka-esque. They looked at me funny. Sigh.

Claire – Hello! You've got a birthday coming up. What would you like?? Gimme hints, woman!

Claire – How UB? Is life as a hardened yet sensitive newspaper journalist keeping you busy and on yer toes? Picked out light fixtures yet? Ya know? I would get more done if I didn't have to be at work for 9 hours of it. Love, Your Firstborn.

Meg – Hey, I was looking in the bookstore today on campus, and they had a copy of a photo book of all the major newspapers' front pages from September 11th and on the front page of the *Journal Sentinel* was a plug for your story. Isn't that cool?

Meg – Dad, I hope you are not going crazy picking out tile and cabinets and faucetry. God knows, I would be. Oh, and I got my physiology test back and got the highest grade in the class!

Meg is finishing her senior year at the University of Notre Dame and waiting for acceptance letters from medical schools. In other words, in the throes of anxiety.

Catherine – Hello darlin Meg. A box from L.L. Bean arrived here with yet another camel toggle coat for you. I assume this is their mistake and that you do not require two identical toggle coats.

Catherine – Meg, get thee a paying summer position. And did you accidentally go back to school with my $100 Ray-Ban sunglasses, which are now MIA? Love, Mother (squinting)

Meg – I'm addressing this only to you, Mom, because it concerns my need for money (which is CONSTANT) and I thought it better to avoid Dad and his grumblings. I'm so defeated when it comes to asking for money, so here goes. I need $129 for football tix and $91 for a parking pass. On a better financial note, I had a good job interview today. When do you leave for NY? Call before then.

Claire – My navy coat is missing buttons. Where the heck do I find buttons in this city?

Catherine – Claire, darling, I just talked to the sheriff's dept, and the first eight digits of your driver's license number are identical to mine, but the threatening letter from the Wisconsin Department of Transportation is your license number, not mine.

Catherine – Meg, darling, I know you have med school interviews, and I just want you to know we love you and admire your diligence in pursuing your goals.

Meg – Mom, could you take a peek upstairs in the bathroom and see if I left facial cleanser? Also, it's my turn to pick the charity for our family's annual Christmas donations, and I chose Doctors Without Borders.

Meg – Hi Mom. You always know the most calming things to say in the most stressful situations. And thanks so much for sending my sandals and the check.

Catherine – Dennis, I love you more than words can say. Thank you so very much for being my Rock of Gibraltar this past year. Happy Valentine's Day!

Dennis – I love you. Always have and always will.

Chapter 14
Not My Boys
September 11, 2002

Trying to come to grips

IS IT ANY wonder that a place called the Yazoo Delta is sweltering in the middle of summer? No.

Like the trip to Death Row, this assignment takes me to a place I never thought I'd be. The story follows four Latino teen girls from Milwaukee who embark on a transformative mission trip to the deep South, witness poverty more profound than their own, and return home wiser and more mature.

I open the story with a description of the small town where they scraped and repainted houses while donating their blood to hordes of ravenous mosquitos. The settlement lays well off the through-road, half-buried in emerald fields of cotton that stretch to the horizon, a dying town almost invisible save for a monolithic gin that closed decades ago. The families who haven't left inhabit primitive "shotgun shacks" or dilapidated mobile homes. In the mornings, toddlers push through squeaky screen doors and make their way to a one-pump filling station that serves as the only general store for miles, where they snack on paint chips curling off the store's wood siding. When their diapers are full, they step out of them and continue on without breaking stride. It is a place thick with heat, humidity, and generations of human misery, and I will never forget the ten days I spent there.

On my first night back in Milwaukee, I take a forty-minute shower and crawl into a familiar bed made with clean sheets, thankful for my life. The following day, I write to a Midwest columnist I know and then to my brother-in-law in New York.

Catherine – Hello my fashionable friend. The Milwaukee Press Club gave me the top award for spot news coverage for the 9/11 story. At first, the *Journal Sentinel* wasn't going to submit my work for consideration. I asked the editor in charge of submissions whether he had ever risked his life for the paper. Then I told him I would nominate myself, and then I'd quit. That rectified the situation. Oh man, this place!

Catherine – Hello Terry. My shrink has ordered me to NY for the 9/11 anniversary. My newspaper, so far, has not. Are you gonna be in town? Can I stay at your place in The Village?

Catherine – Hey Terry, the editors have chosen two reporters to cover the 9/11 anniversary story in New York, and I'm not one of them. It's demoralizing.

Shellie – I know you're getting good advice, but as your friend, I've gotta ask, are you sure it's a good idea to be going to New York alone?

Catherine – Terry, I'm flying to NY on my own.

Claire – It's September 11 again, and I know this time of year is difficult for you. Remember that you always have your family to lean on when times get tough. We love you and we're all proud of you. Take care in New York.

And with that, life takes another turn.

On the first anniversary of the attacks, I am where I want to be, among people who witnessed the tragedy first-hand, who fanned out across the boroughs distributing fliers, who lit candles in Union Square Park. I want to meet the couple who invited me into their warehouse for a respite just long enough to keep me far enough from a tower about to collapse, which saved my life. I want to stand at the brink of Ground Zero and pay my respects to the people who died. So I take vacation days, buy myself a plane ticket, and go alone.

New York is soaked in woe.

Before dawn, bagpipers and drummers begin to march toward the World Trade Center site. At 7:30 a.m., I stand in a huge crowd listening to the first strains of mournful music. A crisp, buffeting wind blows little tornados of dust and grit into the air.

The litany of names continues for hours. At the end, the crowd bursts into thunderous applause. A bugler calls out "Taps." My heart breaks.

I expect to cry. I expect to feel dizzy, nauseous, anxious. I don't. I have come here with a purpose, and somehow I hold myself together long enough to address it.

I convince a police officer to let me through a series of barricades. At a nearby hotel, Paul, the warehouse owner, is attending a function for neighborhood leaders. When he learns I am in the lobby, the door to the meeting room opens and he strides out, arms spread wide. For long moments, we hug one another in the kind of rocking, comforting, tearful embrace of people reunited after a calamity.

After we part, I flag a taxi. I have one more thing to do here. In my purse are pages of one of my notebooks from a year ago, the pages that contain the words of the firefighters I met. The men who sped toward the North Tower a scant twelve minutes before it collapsed.

The firehouse is old, its facade aged by time and weather. Gleaming emergency vehicles line the street out front. Firefighters from across the country have driven to New York to pay their respects to their fallen comrades.

The huge bay doors are open. Dozens of people talk in small groups inside. More stand on the sidewalk and spill out into the street. Briefly, I tell a young officer why I am here. Stunned, he hastens to find his superior.

The fire chief is tall and broad-shouldered with a lantern jaw and thick silver hair. I follow him up a flight of stairs and into a cluttered office. He takes his seat behind a battered wood desk and motions me to a chair facing him. Then he steeples his fingers in front of pursed lips and waits for me to begin.

I introduce myself. I tell him I am a reporter. I tell him I was in New York a year ago.

"I saw a fire truck on the West Side Highway, headed for Ground Zero, going fast. Then it pulled over, and the men jumped down. There was a phone kiosk right there, a public phone, a pay telephone. The guy who got there first put through a call, I guess to his house. I heard what he said. I took down his words. I asked the other guys a couple of questions and took down the answers. Before I knew it, they were on the truck again, heading south. The whole thing took maybe two minutes, at the most."

I tell the fire chief that I would like to give the notebook pages to the firehouse. You could add it to the memorial on display downstairs, I tell him, or give the pages to the families of those men.

He is oddly quiet.

"Here," I say, holding out the pages of the notebook.

The papers in my hand hover over his desk, but he doesn't move.

"You should have this," I say, in what sounds like a plea. "It's a keepsake. It has some of their last words."

He will not touch the offering.

I plow on. "It belongs at the firehouse among the mementos, or with the families."

The chief lowers his gaze. I slump back in the chair, confused.

Finally, he looks up.

"You're wrong," he says, his voice gone to gravel. "Those weren't my boys."

"But they were," I say, leaning forward again, trying to be helpful. "Here, I'll show you."

I flutter the pages. "See? I wrote the number I saw on the side of the truck. It was red, with a white canvas hose coiled on the side. I got the first names they gave me. And that was the route they would have taken, right? And afterward, when the *New York Times* ran all the photos, I recognized them. Sir, I have some of their last words here."

He rises. Chair legs scrape the floor.

"You're mistaken," he says. His face is a stone mask.

My mind spins. I want to tell him that *he* is the one who is wrong, but I lack the courage to contradict him again, and I am beginning to wonder if there's something else going on here.

The chief walks around his desk. I rise, too. He clasps me in a firm, fatherly bear-hug. I start to sob into his shoulder. His breath is fast and shallow. I can feel his heart beating rapidly. The man is chuffing, holding back tears, hiding deep emotion the way men do, those who regard crying as a weakness.

"Try up in Harlem," he says, his voice muffled. "I hear they lost some boys."

And with that, he signals we are done.

He walks me down the stairs and follows me as I thread through the crowd, past mothers and grandmothers hovering over seven-layer salads and pans of brownies, past firefighters from places like Cleveland and Tulsa speaking to one another in low murmurs, past young widows transferring toddlers from one hip to the other, and teenage boys tracing their fingers across the gleaming equipment.

I turn the corner and stop, too stunned to move.

What just happened?

I close my eyes and try to recall the faces of the firefighters I interviewed near Ground Zero a year ago, but time and the protective nature of human memory have conspired to blur their features. Pedestrians veer around me and glance back, curious. Finally, with effort, I hail a taxi.

Back in Milwaukee, back to the familiar routine of home, work, and quick trips to the Hidden Reserve construction site, weeks pass. But the nagging question about what happened at the firehouse—and why—will not go away. One morning, in the pre-dawn haze of awakening, the fire chief crosses my mind again, and I understand.

A news reporter from halfway across the country barged into an anniversary tribute to his fallen heroes. The reporter tells the captain she interviewed his men and watched them drive off and twelve minutes later they died. She has proof. She has their words on paper. She wants the captain to accept her offering, to validate it.

Although the notebook pages bear witness to the humanity of his men, although the pages are a testament to their sacrifice and would be a treasure for the families of the men, the captain will not accept it. To do so, he would have to concede what he regards as unthinkable—that as they raced toward an epic disaster, his heroic "boys" had paused a few moments, a few breaths, a few heartbeats, a few ticks of a forbidden clock, to say goodbye.

Or I am wrong, and the men were from a different firehouse. But I don't think so.

I return the notebooks to the cardboard box where I keep my 9/11 mementos—the vial of dust from the car windshield, an FDNY tee shirt, a few unused Fashion Week show tickets, my newspaper clippings, and the awards I earned. Before I shove the box under my side of our bed, I resolve to find a permanent place for the notebooks so that in the years to come, in a small way, an account of those firefighters that peels back the glossy, single-dimension label of "hero" and reveals their humanity will help tell the story of 9/11.

Notebook, Firefighters

Chapter 15
Motherhood
Autumn, 2002

Don't be idiots

CLAIRE'S EMPLOYER FILES for bankruptcy. She takes the opportunity to register for advanced-degree courses at DePaul University and to search in earnest for the love of her life. Meg is growing penicillin cultures in her dorm room. She has asked me to please send $300 for a deposit on a cruise. She regards it as a Christmas advance.

Meg – I don't have that much money in my account right now. I think I have around $60.

Claire – I'm dating a guy with bad breath. There's no spark. None. Zip. And kissing is OUT of the question. That is the irony of my life. There is a severe drought of decent men in the city this winter. They must be all hibernating because of the cold.

Catherine – Girls, do NOT go outside without a sweater, wool scarf, hat, mittens, Kleenex, warm socks, boots. It is dangerously cold. Do not be idiots. I did not raise idiots.

Claire – Mom, today I am wearing undies, long underwear, camisole, tee shirt, long pants, cardigan, thick socks, tennis shoes, two scarves, long wool coat, hat, ski gloves, lip balm, skin lotion. Feel better now?

Somewhat.

Chapter 16
Florence Nightingale
December 2002

I'd be responsible

DENNIS AND I are wallowing in the splendor of our new home. We've put up a huge Frazier fir tree in the great room, a second one in the Cornelius Vanderbilt study, and a third in the kitchen. I hang wreaths on the doors and stockings on the mantle. Dennis reminds me that in light of our recent expenditures, I'd promised a minimalist Christmas. I bristle—the house looks gorgeous!—and resolve to buy every one of his gifts at Walgreens.

Right after the holidays, I fly down to St. Louis again. Mom can hardly lift her legs. Dad says she goes back to bed right after breakfast. Something's not right down there.

All my recent, spur-of-the-moment trips to St. Louis have prompted my sister and brothers to think of me as a sort of Florence Nightingale meets The Flying Nun, but my willingness to undertake rescue missions began more than a year ago.

Nearly every summer, the Underhills take a trip to the seashore. Some years we headed for Hilton Head. Other years our destination was Sea Island or Kiawah. But our favorite sun and surf spot was Fripp Island, South Carolina. Mom figured these trips would foster a special bond among her six children and, in time, her grandchildren, and they did. Part of the attraction was that Mom almost always rented the beachfront house that Barbara Streisand stayed in during the filming of *The Prince of Tides*, and author Pat Conroy, who wrote the book of the same name, lived right next door.

In July of 2000, Dad was undergoing chemical therapy to treat lymphatic cancer. Mom didn't feel well either, so before they left for the long drive to South Carolina, Mom saw her doctor. He assured her she would feel better in no time.

She did not.

A thousand miles from home, on an island of private beach houses and not much else, she worsened by the day. By the end of the week, she was mostly silent, withdrawing into her pain. The nearest clinic was in the sleepy coastal town of Beaufort, a forty-minute drive from Fripp.

"This is serious," the clinic doctor said. "I can treat her here, or you can get her home immediately, but she needs to be on Prednisone."

He was a young doctor in a three-room clinic in a one-horse Southern town. Mom wanted to talk with her St. Louis doctor. When the man finally took our phone call, he simply said, "Keep your vacation, Merrilee. See me after you get home."

A week later, I was in the newsroom when I got the call from my father.

"Your mother had a little incident last night."

"What happened?"

"Well, she was driving home from the club, and she had to pull over because she couldn't see anything."

"You mean the car lights went out?"

"No. I mean she couldn't see."

"Like, blind?!"

I left work immediately and flew to St. Louis that afternoon. Tom and I drove our mother to St. John's Mercy Hospital. She did not have the flu. She had polymyalgia rheumatica, a painful disorder that inflames muscles and joints. Left untreated, it leads to a severe swelling of blood vessels in the brain, including those that feed the ocular nerves. With mega-doses of Prednisone, doctors saved Mom's sight just in time.

A *Journal Sentinel* friend sends an email. "Where you at? Hanging out with supermodels again?"

Not exactly. Not even remotely.

Now, in the hectic runup to Christmas, 2002, Dr. Donna goes over the risks of a return trip to Thornhill. I tell her I have to go. I still worry all the time about my parents, especially about my mother. If anything happens to them, if one of them falls down a flight of stairs, leaves the stove on and burns down the house, or wanders off without shoes on a winter day, I'd be responsible. It would be my fault for not having asked them more questions when I interviewed them on a street corner, for not delaying them a few critical minutes, just twelve minutes, my fault for closing my notebook and watching their fire truck speed off.

No, wait. That's not right. What I mean is I feel an obligation to be with my parents in St. Louis from time to time, to help monitor their medical care and living conditions.

Chapter 17
Yuma
February 7, 2003

If you get a call, come quick

I'M ON MY way to New York again. My mind should be on the upcoming trends Marc Jacobs, Calvin Klein, and Anne Klein will be showing over the next eight days. It is. But I'm also worried about my parents.

Dad wants to take Mom to visit each of their children one last time. I can't forbid them from doing so, but I'm nervous about them traveling. Nevertheless, he bought airline tickets to Arizona to see Matt and his family. They arrived in Yuma five days ago.

My youngest brother and his wife are great hosts. Visits to their house are filled with easy conversation, Hallmark DVDs, dips in the backyard pool, steaks sizzling on the grill, and prayer.

While I unpack at the Millennium Broadway Hotel, worries about my father's health and stamina occupy my thoughts. These days, I worry about everything. It exasperates Dennis, but I can't help it. For the past couple of years, it seems as if I'm always waiting for something unexpected to happen, always thinking that if I just anticipate it, if I am on the lookout for it and warn others about it, then I can avoid a catastrophe.

It doesn't take a genius to figure out that when a fashion columnist winds up nearly dying in the concussive blast of a felled skyscraper, her perceptions of impending harm will be colored by foreboding.

I sit on the hotel bed beside my open suitcase and stew. My parents are old, and they are sick, and I know a trip to Arizona is too much for them.

On February 9, two days after I arrive in New York, my father suffers a medical crisis. A stroke or heart attack, though it's just a guess. Matt drives him to the Yuma Medical Center. That night, he emails the rest of us.

I am on the other side of America. From now until February 14, I am employed to watch up to five fashion shows each day and write about what I see. Dad's timing sure stinks. Or the timing of Fashion Week stinks. Either way, it's majorly inconvenient for me.

On February 10, we learn that Dad can't put thoughts into words, and his blood is thin on platelets. Ken flies from St. Louis to Arizona.

The next day, Ken writes that Dad's heartbeat is wonky, and that our father went ballistic during an MRI. Ken says Mom's holding up well, but Matt is going to hit a brick wall soon.

Before and after every runway show, I check my phone for messages. What's happening in Yuma seems more real to me than what's traipsing down Bryant Park runways. When I get word that dad's platelet count is lower and that his condition is going downhill, I phone the newsroom to let them know I will have to leave New York early.

None of my siblings understands how torn I have been between my career and my Underhill obligations. Or they don't care. A year ago, the editors denied my request to cover another Fashion Week because of my frequent absences due to family issues. Bailing on this New York trip, the most important recurring assignment of my beat, will not go down well in the newsroom.

But my father is dying. I'm needed. Maybe I can prevent it. I have to try. Should I stay in Manhattan and watch models clomp down the runways?

Paul is in the Caribbean on a sailing trip. He sends word that he will be in and out of Internet service, but reachable via ship-to-shore radio. Pam says it will be difficult for her to be in Arizona due to the dry climate, but she will try to come, and would someone send her the name of a hotel? Matt tells us he has asked God to bless us.

People deal with this type of thing in their own way.

I leave New York, fly to Milwaukee to pack warm-weather clothes, and fly to Yuma. At the door to Dad's hospital room, I pause. He looks melancholy, tired. Doctors can't get his blood platelet levels under control. They think he has Waldenstrom's Macroglobulinemia. The disease has no cure. It will kill him.

Matt's house is a *de facto* hotel for our family. My sister-in-law has made meals, done dishes, washed clothes, changed linens, and kept the walls from falling without a hint that it is a burden to her.

> Claire – I wish I could be there with you right now, but know my thoughts are with you and Grandpa and Grandma. Please let me know if there's anything I can do.

> Catherine – Hi girls. Say your prayers for an easy time for your grandpa and know that he has loved each of you since the day you were born.

On February 20, more than a week after I left New York, Tom and I pick up Pam at the Yuma airport. On the way to the hospital, she falls apart. Arizona is too hot, she says, too dry. She slumps sideways and rests her head against the car window. The air conditioning is on full blast.

Having flown across the country to say goodbye to her desperately ill father, having devoted most of her luggage to a full-sized vaporizer and a sack of optical potions, my emotionally fragile sister wants to turn right around and go home.

But she doesn't. Not yet.

At the hospital, Pam walks purposefully into Dad's room and speaks sweetly into his ear. Afterward, she thumps her forehead against the tiled wall of a corridor, and wails. I try to comfort her, but she waves me off with a slashing arm. Nurses and orderlies find something to do elsewhere.

The following day, Paul is back on dry land and on his way to Arizona.

Dad is worse. He has developed a staph infection in his heart. His kidneys are not functioning. His lungs are congested. A cardiac surgeon offers to do exploratory heart surgery. We bring Mother into the loop, and we all agree—no surgery.

At various times, those I have known all my life surprise me. This is one of those times. While I am silently obsessing over my failure to think of something, anything, that will delay the inevitable and save my father's life, while sirens ring in my ears and visions of a fire truck with a hose coiled neatly on its side zing through my head, and while my brothers grow more and more overwhelmed weighing medical options and differential diagnoses, the most unlikely Underhill of all makes the calmest, wisest, most compassionate decision of all.

Pam.

Pam has been questioning the hospital staff, searching the Internet for information about Waldenstrom's, and talking with the families of other seriously ill patients on the ward. Then she contacts a nearby hospice facility and arranges to have medical personnel transfer Dad to a bed there.

Pam stays long enough to see Dad settled at the hospice in a private room. There is no medical equipment. No blinking monitors or beeping alarms. The lights are dim. The music is soft, soothing.

Pam notices a tray of untouched food beside the bed. She asks a caregiver if she can help Dad eat a little something.

"You can," the nurse says, "but it's more for your peace of mind than anything. His body doesn't want or need food anymore."

Pam tries, God love her. She holds a small spoonful of gelatin to Dad's lips, but it trickles down his chin. It's pitiful.

Within the hour, she is in a taxi bound for the Yuma airport.

I sit in a corner of the hospice room, lost in thought.

For years, all of us have understood that our sister . . . what? Ken, too. We who have known them since their earliest days have stood by as their childhood quirks became patterns of behavior that should have triggered alerts. Pam and Ken weren't quirky children; they were kids with dissimilar but serious conditions, disorders that were not addressed. Not diagnosed. Not treated. Not given a name, and not overcome. This wasn't the job of their siblings. It was the job of their parents, their teachers, the family doctor, the parish priests who set themselves up as family counselors. All of them failed our sister and brother. From their childhood on, Pam and Ken struggled unassisted, and yet they completed a university education, forged relationships and careers, married, bought homes, and reared good children. How they managed, I'll never know.

My phone rings. Another call from the newsroom. "We hope you and your family are holding up as well as you can," the editor says, adding pointedly, "We'll look forward to seeing you Tuesday."

Oh God, the *Journal Sentinel* Spring Fashion Section. I was supposed to start on that right after the runway shows.

There are times when life has razor-sharp edges.

I board a plane bound for Milwaukee, thoughts spinning about clothes, models, makeup, and hair, and the "look" of another Spring Fashion Section. It should be a two-week process. I make it happen in four days. Then I hurry back to Yuma.

Watching our mother watch her husband slip away is a torment. And the irony of where this is happening is lost on none of us. Dad was born and reared on the East Coast. He loved the snap of taut sails over open water, the scent of mowed grass, the rustling of autumn cornfields during country walks with his dog. He was a man deeply rooted in the Midwest, and yet he will take his final breath in a desert.

A hospice nurse tells us that some patients on the brink of death experience a period of cognition, become alert.

"It's brief," the nurse says. "If you get a call, come quick."

The call comes in deep night. The hospice is eerily quiet. At the doorway to Dad's room, we leave the harsh, chemical light of fluorescent fixtures and enter the dusky space. He's lying on his side, facing the door, plucking at the bedclothes.

"Oh," he says. He struggles to lever up on an elbow, but it's too much. He's too weak.

We disperse around the bed, surround him with our love. Mom and Matt stand on one side. I don't want to crowd, so I move to the other side of the bed. Too late, I realize Dad is facing away from me. I do not think he realizes I'm in the room.

We speak to him in low murmurs, saying the things people say. We love you. It's okay to go now. We will take care of everything.

Matt says a prayer.

Dad's eyes are filmy but open. Eventually, we fall silent and simply stand in place, a vignette rendered in shades of grief. I seesaw from anxiety to morbid thoughts. Where are the doctors? Why isn't anyone helping him? But the hospice staff *is* helping. I realize that. They're helping him die in peace and leave the world with dignity.

Still, my head is pounding. I smell the faint scent of a jet fuel fire. I dare not look up. Death is in the room, tingling my skin, raising the hairs at the base of my skull just like the morning I looked up to a bluebell sky and saw people try to fly on wings of fire.

Then what cannot be, happens: Dad reaches out a dry, clawed hand to his wife of fifty-three years. She bends over the bedrail and clasps his hand in both of hers. Dad looks up at her. In a voice so high and reedy I hardly recognized it, he says, "Be a good girl."

The effort exhausts him, but he is not done. He reaches for Matt, takes the hand of his son, the last of his six children, and says, "Be a good boy."

Simple words by which to live a worthy life, offered with a man's last breaths. *Be good. Be good.*

Chapter 18
Haven
March 2003

Every room is trashed

MY SISTER-IN-LAW PREPARES a lovely dinner. We thought we had no appetite, but we are wrong. After we clear the dishes, we shuffle to the family room and collapse on sofas and soft chairs. Mom gets the chair that rocks. Her bones are brittle. Every inch of her hurts. It's hard to tell how long her mind holds a thought.

Matt pops *South Pacific* in the DVD player. It's one of Mom's favorites, something to pass the time. For a while, Mom appears to be enjoying the show and following its themes. The rest of us stare at the screen, unseeing. When Mitzi Gaynor plops on a driftwood log and starts singing "I'm in Love with the Most Wonderful Man," I glance over at Mom and realize she's agitated.

"Mother?"

Her eyes well up with tears.

"Mom? Honey?"

She doesn't answer. Her cheeks flush. She looks more miserable by the moment. Finally, she cries out, "Where's Dad?"

If any of us are still in doubt about our mother's cognition, it is clear now.

After we put her to bed, we try to figure out what to do. In the short run, she will need one of her children with her and assistance with bathing, dressing, and grooming. I agree to take a leave of absence from the *Journal Sentinel* and stay in St. Louis with Mom until full-time, round-the-clock home care is in place.

That night, a familiar phrase drifts into my thoughts:

Surely the worst is over.

It is not.

When it became clear that our father would not linger long, Tom returned to St. Louis to check on Thornhill and start funeral arrangements. Now, as we pack for the funeral in St. Louis, Tom phones. Matt hands the phone to me. Tom doesn't seem to know where to start; but if there's one thing a career in newspaper journalism has taught me, it's how to ask questions and get answers. Eventually, my brother reveals his devastating news.

It was a raw, lead-sky, late February morning. The minute Tom opened the front door at Thornhill, he smelled something horrible. By the time he got to the kitchen, the odor was overpowering. Someone had smeared baked beans, peaches in syrup, and mushroom soup across the countertops. Pickles and olives, jelly and mayonnaise spattered the floor. Crushed breakfast cereal, crackers, and chips soaked in milk covered the dinette table and drizzled down onto chairs.

Tom was more angry than worried; he figured Ken had gone to the house while Mom and Dad were in Yuma, made a big lunch, and left before he cleaned up the kitchen. Tom wiped everything down and left the kitchen spotless.

The following day, Tom returned to the house. When he opened the front door, there was the smell again. And in the kitchen was the same awful mess as before.

Then, Tom heard a noise.

The door between the kitchen and the family room was ajar. From across the kitchen, Tom realized somebody was hiding behind the door, hiding in a house littered with food and reeking of something far worse. Tom took a few steps toward the door and yelled, "What are you doing here?"

A man mumbled, "They told me I could stay here."

"Who told you?"

"Don't know."

Now Tom was worried. He backtracked through the house, out the front door, and down the brick walk to his car. As he was dialing 911 on his cell phone, he saw the intruder leave the house and disappear around a corner of the garage. When the police arrived, Tom told them he thought the guy ran down the steep hill to the creek, crossed over to the broad meadow, and made his way up the wooded hill to Manchester Road.

Tom followed the officers while they searched the house.

"Cath, every room is trashed," he told me on the phone. "And when I say trashed, I mean trashed way beyond what a home burglar would do looking for valuables. This is somebody looking to destroy the house. What he did was bad, Cath. Feces rubbed all over, even in the master bedroom."

The police concluded that the intruder had wandered out to the suburbs from one of the city's shelters. When he found himself in unfamiliar territory, he searched for a warm, dry place to sleep, a place where no one would find him. Mom and Dad never lock anything, not doors, not cars, not Mom's jewelry box. It was beyond foolhardy; it was dangerous.

The weather in St. Louis had been cold, damp, and dreary. Police surmised the man had lifted the overhead garage door and slept in Dad's Jeep a few nights. Then the man tried the door to Dad's den and walked right in. Police think he was inside a week.

Officers found the man walking along the shoulder of Manchester Road and took him into custody. One of them told Tom he'd been lucky the man didn't have a loaded gun or a knife. Tom doesn't sound like a lucky guy. Who can blame him? His father has just died. His mother is in frail health. He was supposed to be at work, supposed to be arranging a funeral Mass and burial, supposed to be contacting our parents' friends and our distant relatives. His mother's house is unlivable. His clothing reeked.

When he left Thornhill that afternoon, Tom drove straight to his condominium three miles away. He took a scalding shower and then picked up from the floor the clothes he wore that day, walked outside, and dumped them in a trash can. An officer had warned him it was likely that residue in the house had contaminated his clothes with hepatitis spores.

Chapter 19
Dads Wore Hats
1950s – 1980s

Rounded at the corners

ON THE NIGHT my father died, the night we realized my mother is incapable of independent living, the night we learned an intruder had defiled her home, *our* home, the night I resolve to subordinate the career I love for the family I love more, I take half of a sleeping pill. Minutes later, I swallow the other half. I figure that and a glass of wine might stave off the sweat-drenched nightmares I fear are coming.

Eventually, I fall asleep humming, "If I Could Turn Back Time." That night, I dream about my early childhood. We lived in Chafford Woods, a neighborhood about ten miles west of downtown St. Louis. Moms wore skirts back then. They hung laundry on clotheslines and made meatloaves. Dads wore hats, pushed lawnmowers with whirring blades, built hillocks of charcoal briquettes to barbecue hamburgers, raked leaves into piles in the street and watched them burn to ashes. Everybody knew everybody.

In my dream, it was winter, and me and my Chafford Woods pals had lugged our sleds to a nearby hilltop so we could collide with one another on purpose on the way down. Then it was summer, and we were playing kickball in the street and skipping in the foggy wake of the mosquito man's truck. Finally, it was a rainy Saturday morning, and Paul, Tom, and I were dragging blankets into a nook under the eaves and constructing elaborate domiciles for ourselves, which we called cover-houses.

In my second dream that night, Mom and Dad announced at our dinner table in Chafford Woods that a new little Underhill was on the way and that we would all move to a big new house soon. In protest, I went off solid food for an hour, and when that didn't reverse my parents' plans, I resigned myself to a flawed life.

I woke with a start. It was five in the morning, too early for anyone else to be up, too late for me to try and go back to sleep. While I finished packing for the trip to St. Louis, I thought about our early years at Thornhill.

The two-acre parcel my father bought in the fall of 1959 was at the far edge of St. Louis County, an intangible line where platted residential developments encroached on rural Missouri. I was eleven years old and heartbroken at the prospect of moving away from Chafford Woods and everything familiar. I took to disparaging Thornhill Estates the only way I could think of: I called it Outer Mongolia. Ours was the third house to go up. Eventually, there would be a hundred and twenty homes on lots measured by the acre, a horse stable, paved tennis courts, a deep-water pool, a shallow children's pool, a brick changing house. But in the early days, those amenities had not been started, and there was little to distinguish future homesites from hills, meadows, and woodlands.

Carpenters were still installing flooring in our new house when the Underhills came to stay. That first night, I cried myself to sleep. In the morning, I sat on our new brick stoop and glowered at our front yard, a long, sloping swathe of rock-riddled dirt.

"Cath, c'mon!" It was Paul. "We found a creek at the bottom of the hill. There's a baby duck, and Tommy saw a beaver!"

A beaver! Now that's something.

And so it began.

That summer, we splashed in the clear-running stream at the bottom of the hill, squealing as slithery things tickled our ankles. We searched the shoals for arrowheads and carried our treasures home in cupped hands. We ate bologna-sandwich picnics in a meadow dotted with Queen Anne's Lace, tamped trails in thigh-high grass, built forts in thickets. One day, I glimpsed a red fox. He eyed me warily and pranced away.

On any given day, our new house sang with the laughter of my sister on the telephone, the muffled thumps of my brothers roughhousing on a couch, the rasp of a dog bowl licked across the kitchen floor, and the cheers of Cardinal fans at a game broadcast over the radio. Almost from the beginning, the rooms were scented with the aromas of morning bacon and cinnamon rolls, late-night pipe smoke, and treacly hair spray. After a rain, the distinctive odor of damp tube socks and wet dog prevailed.

Eventually, the family living on the farm just west of our property sold its land to the Thornhill developer. Soon, we saw architects, builders, and landscapers pace off the farmer's corduroyed fields, and watched the line between exurban and rural retreat a little farther. Next, surveyors appeared down by the creek. Men with clipboards pounded orange stakes into the flower-flecked meadow and trampled the tasseling grass. Before long, the paths the Underhill kids blazed when we first discovered the novelties of life in Outer Mongolia had vanished.

In my coming-of-age years at Thornhill, I learned from my father how to wash a skunk-sprayed dog with tomato juice, how to wait on a sinking curveball, operate a power drill, use an Allen wrench, open a pocketknife, clean a paintbrush, and wrap an odd-shaped package for mailing. He taught me how to plunge a toilet, light a barbecue fire, extinguish a sparkler, toggle a circuit breaker, set a thermostat, fill a car's gas tank, and balance a checkbook. He instructed his children about how to fold an American flag, and why.

My mother taught me everything I know about folding fitted sheets, hand-washing delicates, and achieving a decent home manicure. She emphasized the importance of a well-written thank you note and the small efforts that contribute to gracious entertaining. Her kitchen was more practical than fancy, but it was large enough to prepare meals for a family of eight every night, bake loaves of yeast bread on wintry Saturday mornings, make strawberry rhubarb pies on Spring afternoons and Bundt cakes on birthdays.

My early years were not all hearts and roses. My mother went into sulks prompted by problems we kids couldn't fix or even figure out. And at least once a week, one of us did something to send Dad into orbit, and he delivered a leather-belt spanking that hurt for hours.

But mostly, I remember my early childhood in pastel shades, soft and rounded at the corners.

During the flight to St. Louis, I went to work on a writing project, and although it was not an assignment from an editor, I found myself wishing in a way that it was.

Major news organizations archive the life stories of politicians, celebrities, and virtually anyone else of note so that, when an important person dies, a pre-written obituary will be available, one that only needs a succinct update.

Seated on a plane next to my silent, devastated mother, both of us aware the crew has stowed a casket in the luggage bay below us, I take up a pen. Good thing I have experience at writing on deadline. As soon as we take off, I begin the eulogy I will give in a couple of days for my father. I finish it shortly before we touch down in St. Louis.

Chapter 20
Eulogy
March 2003

He served with honor

THE FAMILY MY father left behind is in shambles. Dementia has diminished his widow. She suffers from excruciating spinal stenosis and the first signs of lung disease. She needs immediate, permanent 'round the clock care.

Pam, the elder daughter, is unreliable, melodramatic, and increasingly agoraphobic. Paul, the eldest son, is in Oregon. I am dealing with Post-Traumatic Stress Disorder and a crumbling career. Tom is trying to forget his confrontation with the Thornhill intruder. Ken's marriage is strained, his employment record is unstable, and we suspect he is abusing street drugs. Matt is exhausted.

It is a wrenching homecoming.

Mom and I go straight from the St. Louis airport to a Marriott Hotel five miles from Thornhill. Although we describe to Mother in the vaguest terms why she cannot go back to Thornhill immediately, she is devastated. On the day of the funeral, she is too sick, weak, distressed, and in pain to attend the services. One of her friends stays with her at the hotel.

What a crying shame.

Eulogy for My Father[12]

Once there was a scrappy little boy, a New Yorker who came to the Midwest to study engineering and so loved St. Louis that he would not leave. He was an only child who wanted a big family so that his house would sing with the sound of boys shooting hoops on the driveway, hairdryers whirring in upstairs bedrooms, with sleepover giggles and doorbells and dog barks, jangling phones and soothing piano music, clattering pots, sloshing clothes washers, humming dryers.

Once, there was a handsome young man from White Plains, New York, who enlisted in the United States Navy during wartime, a groom who couldn't get to the church on time because his ship was at sea. A young man who served with honor aboard a minesweeper, dangerous duty, helping win a world war so that future generations might live in peace.

Once there was a young husband and father who raced a sluggish sailboat on summer Sundays, hoping for a puff of wind. Who came home after a long day at the office, on a construction site, or on the road, took his seat at the head of the supper table, removed his napkin from its silver ring, pointed to one of his children to say grace, and then regaled us all with a joke or story. He was the first to laugh at his punch line. A man who, in the full of life, made Whiskey Sours after church on Christmas. Who swore lightly when the occasion warranted and prayed to St. Michael often.

On summer Saturdays, he would coax his riding mower to life and close-crop an acre of grass, return to the house in the late afternoon spangled with clippings. Shower, shave, and put on clean clothes for the table.

Once there was an engineer, a baseball fan, a dog lover, a John Wayne admirer, morning newspaper reader, Jeep driver, family ancestry recorder, teacher of chess to children, kitchen gardener with zucchini to spare, an election-day voter, Sunday worshiper, midnight sandwich maker, a son, a husband, a dad, a patriot. A man who named each of his bird dogs Patsy. An honest man.

Like all of us, my dad had his faults. He chewed tobacco and spat the slurry into a cup he kept near his favorite chair. He bottled up whatever he didn't want to remember (or divulge) about his past and sealed it tight. But his merits far outweighed his faults.

In autumn, he baked apple pies and gave them to neighbors who were surprised and delighted in equal doses. In winter, he simmered huge batches of beef stew and drove into the city to deliver them to a meal center for the poor. On Sunday nights in the dead of winter, Dad took my sister and me to school-sponsored dances ten miles from Thornhill, and was there, waiting, when the last song ended. In summer, he coached my brothers' baseball teams from the sidelines of sunbaked, bald-dirt diamonds.

He did not go to movie theaters, but he loved watching movies on late-night television. His final tally on *Run Silent, Run Deep* was in the double-digits. He admired Delores del Rio. I always suspected he was smitten with Angie Dickinson.

In his later years, Dad was notorious for begging off Christmas Eve Mass due to "stomach trouble," a convenient ailment that miraculously vanished in time for him to meet us at his favorite Italian restaurant on the Hill, for a meal that began with toasted ravioli and ended with cannoli.

In the last years of his life, he would whistle after supper for his dog, a hellion of a German shorthair he named Heidi because she did not deserve the honorarium he had given his four previous English Pointers, all named

Patsy. In his basement workroom at Thornhill, where it was cool in summer and sweater-weather in winter, he would stand at a high wood table and motion for the dog to flop on a scrap of carpet at his feet. On those nights, the strains of big-band music rose through the heat vents from a transistor radio he propped inside the window well. With a slide rule, a steady hand, and the patience of Job, he built three handsome model ships, Gloucester schooners with soaring masts, webbed rigging, and impossibly small cleats and winches. He intended to make six, an heirloom gift for each of his children, but he was taken after completing three.

Once there was a father who summoned his children one by one—and in time his grandchildren—to a marble chess table in front of his fireplace. He bade them listen as he revealed the names of the figures on the table, described the powers and deficiencies of each small brass piece and revealed the strategies of the game. He warned that the castles are sturdy but the knights are brave. He admonished us to protect the king at all costs, and to not rely exclusively on castles, horses, or legions of pawns, for they will be swept from the field, but with the queen. Even in defeat, he said, there is victory for a king with a queen at his side.

After the funeral Mass, we make the slow drive to Resurrection Cemetery in South St. Louis. Pam arranged for a Navy officer to play "Taps" at the cemetery. When the time comes, he draws a bugle to his lips, and the haunting, twenty-four-note bugle call rings out into the stone-gray day.

Behind us, an old tree spreads its limbs over obelisks and marble angels. Sunlight angles through its branches, casting milky beams onto the red granite headstone my parents selected years earlier, a marker inscribed with the name UNDERHILL.

Chapter 21
Redress
2003

The nights come early

WALL-TO-WALL CARPETING ripped up. Curtains and draperies thrown away. Sheets, pillows, and mattresses pitched. Floors scoured. Windows washed. Replacement wardrobe for an eighty-three-year-old widow with a crumbling spine, in progress.

One of my brothers suggests I stay in St. Louis with Mom until March 20. I bite my tongue.

Does anyone in this family realize how long I have been away from my job? Do they even care?

I sit in a Marriott hotel room and stew, knowing I will stay on and trying to decode why I repeatedly put the career I love in jeopardy.

I must enjoy the role of the Sacrificial Sibling. Or I like being needed. Maybe I just want to be saintlier than my siblings or enjoy griping about being a saint. The reality is I'm so hollowed by the death of my father that holing up in a pleasant hotel with my mother seems preferable to the creative responsibilities and deadline pressures of a newsroom.

I suggest Mother come up to Milwaukee and stay with Dennis and me until Thornhill is habitable. Paul nixes it. He says she won't adapt to new surroundings, new doctors, and separation from her friends. He's got a point.

One of my Features Department friends sends an email. He says the editors are wondering when I might return. Another friend from the paper emails, too. "There's a big empty spot where you sit," she says.

I can hardly bear to think about fashion trends and supermodels. What, exactly, would happen to my mother if I leave before Thornhill is habitable or before this family has a competent caregiver on board?

Dennis accuses me of always being on the lookout for something terrible to happen. It's pretty true. The term is "hypervigilance." That and the term "trauma-related guilt" are symptoms of PTSD. I have to admit I'm often on the lookout for unexpected danger, and I wonder if guilt is motivating me to save my fragile mother, but from what?

Ah, well, all that requires more introspection than I can deal with right now.

March 20 comes and goes. The Marriott feels more like home than my home.

Matt has lined up his sister-in-law to stay with Mom at Thornhill as soon as the house is ready and until we find a permanent arrangement.

Tom is supervising the professional clean-up of the house. Paul is dealing with property insurance issues, pharmacy bills, Dad's will, and Mom's taxes. Pam and Ken are researching senior centers and home care agencies. Matt is getting his life back. I am with Mom.

I miss Dennis. The days are long. The nights come early.

Pam emails. She's finishing thank-you notes. Did Mom's first cousins once removed send a porcelain bowl to the funeral home?

Tom emails. He's writing thank you notes, too. Should "father" be capitalized?

Meg writes. She had a fantastic time in the Bahamas, and will tell me all about it when I get back to Milwaukee.

Claire writes. She's glad Grandma liked her gift.

I write. I tell my sister and brothers that Dad's infested Jeep was towed off yesterday and the towing guy refused to touch the interior of the car. I tell them the carpet cleaners wrecked the living room Oriental rug. I let them know their mother has asked 45,000 times what the heck happened to her Cadillac. I tell them somebody needs to go out and buy Mom a car.

At the end of March, Matt's sister-in-law arrives. I return to Milwaukee and slam back to work the following day.

> Catherine – Claire, honey, are you still going to Toronto?
> Significant outbreak of SARS has hit Toronto. Travel restrictions.
> Love, Your ever-vigilant Mother.
>
> Claire – Motherrrr! You are fibbing, and to be honest, it's no
> different than the regular flu. My shoulder hurts. Love you,
> mom. PS had a job interview. Went well.

Paul tells us it would break his heart to rush to install Mom in a senior center. He views his role as protector of her wishes but emphasizes that none of us is solely in charge, which is odd because he sure writes like he's in charge.

There's more. It isn't pretty.

Toward the end of his email, he refers to the incident in Dad's den the day I abruptly left Thornhill. Although he wasn't there, although he knows few of the details, Paul says I intruded on Dad's authority, received a harsh reaction from Dad, and "laid low" for a year.

Reading his words, I broke down and cried.

If any of my brothers had been there on that awful day, they would have slugged our father. And I did not "lay low" afterward; I was working full-time. I was filing dispatches from the scene of a monumental terrorist attack. I was winning awards. I was building a house. I was in therapy for depression, suicidal inclinations, and a double-whammy of PTSD.

I was surviving.

> Ken – Paul, you fucked up. Your two-page rant at all of us, especially your sister Cathy, was inexcusable. I suggest you apologize to everyone so that we can move on to more constructive discussions.
>
> I also want to point out that your email made not one single mention of a workable solution to the fact that we will not have full-time care for Mom in a matter of weeks, if not days. And I haven't read or heard you make any offer to dig in here in St. Louis, give up a month, or whatever it takes. Your sister Cathy had offered to do that (for the second time!).

I took a leave of absence from the *Journal Sentinel* and returned to St. Louis April 21. Except for a long weekend in mid-May for Notre Dame University's graduation, I stayed a month at Thornhill caring for my mother. By that time, I hope we will have found a permanent solution to her living situation.

Ken offers to have Mom move in with him and Tina providing we hire a daytime caregiver.

Mom is erratic. One day she cleans and polishes silver and asks to go to Blockbuster for a Christopher Plummer movie. The next day she spends hours staring blankly and asking the same question repeatedly. She is terrified of being sent to a nursing home, and desperate for us to hire a permanent home companion for her. After a good cry, she tells me she wants to send back one of the new chairs because it's too big for the family room.

Chapter 22
Pecking Order
Spring 2003

I discovered the truth

MY SIBLINGS AND I are as distinct from one another as leaves on a tree. And yet, the identities we forged at Thornhill are as fixed today as they were almost a half-century ago.

Pam is the oldest and least suited to be. My sister is intelligent and studious, perceptive, and good-hearted. But from her earliest years, my sister has come unwound over issues we would have shrugged off. Growing up, she did not stand out socially and seemed secure only when she was among a small circle of girlfriends who had known one another since kindergarten.

In time, her marriage to Peter ended, but her career as creative director of the public relations firm founded by her former husband was solid and fulfilling.

By the time of Dad's last illness, Pam was living alone in Ithaca and increasingly agoraphobic. Her contributions to family problems consisted of what she could do from Ithaca. But she was secure, financially. A buyer had made a fabulous offer for the firm, but there was a hitch. Peter and Pam must complete a last, large project, one that called for eloquent writing. Pam was in a bind: None of her best freelance writers was available. Desperate, she phoned me. She begged me to quit my full-time job at the *Journal Sentinel* and go to work for her. She said I could work from home. She said she would pay me a salary higher than I was getting from the paper. She said the position was permanent. She warned me that I would have to complete the first writing project on a tight deadline. She said she was confident I could do it.

My sister did not reveal that she and Peter would no longer own the company, or have anything to do with it after the project finished. Although I had no way of knowing I would be hung out to dry, I had qualms about leaving a job I loved and going to work for my phlegmatic sister. Dennis was flat against it.

I turned her down.

Pam found a different writer. Peter sold the company. The price was in the millions of dollars.

I heard the news through the family grapevine and was stunned to discover my sister had asked me to leave an award-winning newspaper career for a one-time writing assignment.

I tell her I don't want to hear from her again. Afterward, I swim in pools of guilt but do nothing to repair the breach.

I realize my sister is ill. We all do. I tell myself that she has three adult children. I tell myself I have no training in counseling. I convince myself I am relieved to be done with Pam.

How mistaken I am.

Chapter 23
Revolving Door
Late Spring 2003

All of us, together again

DENNIS IS ADJUSTING to life in the exurbs. He especially likes the wildlife in Hidden Reserve. In Whitefish Bay, he battled squirrels, geese, skunks, and raccoons that upturned our trash bins and scattered detritus into the alley. In Hidden Reserve, he sees hawks, owls, and a red fox. A mother deer and her fawn prance along our back property line. A blue heron makes its warm-weather home in the nearby wetlands.

Everything about Hidden Reserve reminds me of my years at Thornhill. But in truth, the Thornhill house is a sad place now. Weeds fill the gardens. Bedrooms echo with a hollow emptiness. Prescription bottles, lists of emergency contacts, and elder-care instructions clutter the dinner table, where once my father stood for a prayer of thanksgiving before carving a ham or meatloaf to feed his hungry boys and girls.

In mid-April, Paul tells us he has researched elder care agencies, and he recommends a company called Compassion & Care. He estimates the after-tax cost will be $4,500 a month.

The six of us make plans to meet at Thornhill. Pam forwards flight dates and makes sure we understand they are fixed in stone. If she is aware of anyone else's time constraints or obligations, she gives no evidence of it.

I drive from Milwaukee to St. Louis through rain and wind for seven hours. Paul is already at Thornhill. He is starting the fifth interview with care agency staffers when I arrive. Before the weekend is out, he will have interviewed several more. Some have yet to master subject-verb agreement. Others are oblivious to the canyon between those who regard "ain't" as a multi-use verb and those who restrict it to recitations of *Tom Sawyer*.

Mom is docile, probably because she has all six of us back in St. Lou. For her, it's like reliving the 1960s.

When she asks us to make a formal dinner and serve it in the dining room, we sink a little at the effort, and then we make it happen. With candles glowing and flowers blooming and crystal glinting and silver shining, the lesser Underhills scrunch together on both sides of the table. Mom takes her traditional place at the end of the table close to the kitchen. It's so good to see her beaming. It could be the wine and pain meds.

Paul claims the seat at the far end of the table. Dad's place.

Could he have left the chair empty?

The following day, Paul says he intends to grill salmon. I plan to grill Paul about the scope of his powers in the family.

> Meg – While in MKE, I snuck a peek in your closet and saw those adorable polka dot shoes and matching sweater! That's the kind of stuff I usually get to talk to you about when I'm home but haven't gotten a chance to. Telling Dad I like your polka dot shoes doesn't produce the same effect. Miss you, Mom.

Paul has hired Compassion & Care. The first C&C caregiver has arrived. All is well.

All is not well.

I phone Thornhill from Milwaukee and have a nice chat with Mother when she lowers her voice. "One of the new caregivers is hovering." Paul bristles. He hired the woman. He says she worked at St. John's Mercy Hospital for years and knows about Mom's medical needs. It occurs to me that hovering and being knowledgeable are not mutually exclusive.

In late spring, Ken reports that Mom doesn't like Veronica. Also, Veronica does not drive.

I asked, "And Veronica is who, exactly?"

In May, Paul flies to St. Louis to be with Mom when she undergoes kyphoplasty, a surgery intended to relieve the pain of spinal compression fractures. Afterward, Paul says there isn't a great deal of improvement in her level of pain.

Chapter 24
Blessings
May 2003

Mile-long legs and a wardrobe of miniskirts

ISSUES AT THORNHILL are simmering.

C&C tells us that Ronnie will be on the job only one more night. I deduce that Ronnie is Veronica, the non-driving caregiver. Sahba will be a long-term sub while Jean (Jeanne?) recuperates. We wonder if Jean (Jeanne?) is the hospitalized patient with gall bladder problems.

Ken has concerns. He tells us Sahba, the temporary replacement for Jean/Jeanne (gall bladder), went into fairly graphic detail about her horrific childhood in Iran when the Shah was overthrown, and that Mom was uncomfortable.

Jean/Jeanne is still in intensive care. A replacement, Tatiana, is from Russia or Ukraine, or one of the "stans," a willowy brunette with mile-long legs and a wardrobe of miniskirts.

Tom contacts me. He says he's unsure what the caregiver situation is.

Join the club, Tom.

One morning when I phone my mother from Milwaukee, she does not know the caregiver's name in her home. I ask Mother to put the woman on the line. When I ask her name, she replies, "Krissie." I do not know her last name. Mother does not even know her first name. Krissie has been on the job for a total of three hours and forty-six minutes.

Krissie tells me that Jean/Jeanne is still ill, and C&C has canned Ronnie/Veronica, and Bernadette quit after three days, which is hardly surprising. Bernadette had just re-entered the world at large after two years in a cloistered convent. Tatiana, the beautiful Ukrainian whose English is less than intelligible, is taking tonight's shift.

According to the well-informed Krissie, Angel had the day shift yesterday.

"Who had the night shift?" I ask.

Krissie replies, "The Ukrainian woman."

I ask Ken what the hell is going on down there.

He says the agency is scrambling. Nobody knows from one day to the next who will be caring for our mother. He says our family is trying to buy diamonds from a gumball machine.

Chapter 25
The Beginning of the End
Early June 2003

Someone is watching

ON JUNE 9, THE dean of a Milwaukee college approaches me with an offer: Would I teach a fashion course in the fall? I take the proposal to my editors, and after a couple of discussions, I am approved to accept the offer.

Meanwhile, someone, somewhere, is watching.

Chapter 26
Lapses
Late June 2003

A serious problem

I REMEMBER THE month, but not the day of the week. I remember the anguished minutes, but not the pivotal hour.

For centuries, experts have studied the process of remembering, and yet precisely how it works, they cannot say.

The process of forgetting is well understood. We forget things as a result of traumatic head injuries. Or because we store the memory or experience so deep within the brain that we have trouble retrieving it. Or because we only glancingly noted it in the first place. Or because the memory we are trying to recover is at odds with another memory, and they cancel one another. We forget things because we have grown old. We forget because we *want to, have to, need to*. In such cases, remembering is so psychologically damaging than being unable or unwilling to do so is an act of self-preservation.

After my swift and dramatic fall from grace, I forget details too painful or insignificant to remember. The day of the week. The time of day. Most of what occurred, though, is carved into my heart. Some of it, with varying degrees of accuracy, is published, public record.

I remember an editor taking me to a conference room, closing the door, questioning me, and taking notes about my answers. When the editor ends her list, she leaves the conference room and closes the door. I sit long minutes, worrying. I know I am in trouble, but I do not understand why or realize how deeply.

After an eternity, the editor returns and beckons to me. We walk in silence to an office in the main newsroom. At least four editors and a representative of the Milwaukee Newspaper Guild Local 51 are in the small room. I take the only empty chair. The senior editor questions me calmly but pointedly about the sources for material in my stories. Quickly, he focuses on a story I wrote after I returned from St. Louis, published in early June. It was a feature of about thirty paragraphs tracing the history of bikini bathing suits.[13]

The editor says someone has informed the *Journal Sentinel* about a serious problem with my story. He does not say who brought the issue to his attention.

I do not ask. The union representative takes out a pencil and starts to fill pages of a notebook.

The editor says an initial analysis of the reporting shows that the tenth paragraph of my story is an almost word-for-word repetition of another writer's published work, with no attribution. The eleventh paragraph of my story begins with more complete attribution: "Writer Steve Rushin, whose paean to the tiny two-piece appeared in *Sports Illustrated*'s 1997 swimsuit edition, picks up the story from there."

But after that, my story continues with material researched and written by others. Aside from one sentence that begins with "One writer said . . ." and another sentence that begins with "In 1957, *Modern Girl Magazine* sniffed . . ." I did not attribute anything else in my story to another source. I left the impression that the facts and how I presented them originated with me.

Plagiarism.

My blood runs cold.

The meeting is brief. More questions. More attempts by me to break through a crushing daze and answer. Bewildered, sickened, and ashamed, I apologize. The editor says the paper will conduct a further examination of my work.

Allen, the union representative, volunteers to escort me from the building. He is somber but kind. To minimize my exposure to the curious stares of a newsroom that is now all eyes, he suggests we take a service exit the janitors use. On the far side of its unmarked door, I pause, unsure if my knees will support me. The lighting is harsh. The walls are bare. I glance down into the shadowy stairwell. Flights of steps angle along each side of the square pit until they end four gritty stories below. I grip the steel-pipe railing and begin my descent. My head is swimming. On the ground floor, Allen makes sure I am outside the building before he goes back to retrieve my purse from my desk. The service door closes behind him. I hear the lock click.

Out on the sidewalk, I blink into city traffic, too stunned to move. *What now?*

I have no distinct memory of driving home. I presume I broke down in tears and phoned Dennis. He probably had to work through the afternoon, so I would have been alone for several hours. During that time, my thoughts would have returned time and again to the moment I paused on a gritty landing, stared down into the dark void of a cement stairwell, and saw my future.

The *Journal Sentinel* runs a brief Editor's Note stating that the bikini story contained unattributed material.

By early July, when I have heard nothing from the paper, Dennis hires an employment lawyer. I see no point in it. By then, I have cast off the PTSD symptom most appealing to me—avoidance. I know in my heart that I am entirely to blame.

I should have seen the extent to which I allowed Underhill issues to subordinate my professional life. I should have seen how that stifled my talent and creativity. Should have acknowledged it was hubris that led me to assume I could excel at dueling, demanding roles. Should have minimized my participation in Underhill family matters. Should have taken an extended leave of absence from work far sooner.

Had there not been so much turmoil in my personal life, and for so long, had I not assumed I was the only one who could set things to right, would I have written other peoples' work as if it were my own? Maybe. Maybe not. I'll never know. It doesn't matter now.

But here's what I do know: I should have quit working long ago, should have resigned with my reputation intact.

Friends from the *Journal Sentinel* send emails assuring me that they miss me. I answer every note, trying for a gracious tone even though I fall deeper into a well of shame and despair with each new note.

> Catherine – What an uplifting note you sent today. I was afraid
> I would never again hear my name and the word "admire"
> and "respect" in the same sentence. Thank you. It's incredibly
> heartening to hear that I have friends downtown who are in my
> corner.

Meg is home for the summer. She invites five friends from her Notre Dame days for the long July Fourth weekend. Cans of beer chill in the fridge. Hamburgers sizzle on the grill. Fireworks bloom in the night sky. It's a temporary tonic, a welcome diversion that pauses the carousel of thoughts spinning in my head about my lost career.

Chapter 27
Editors
1970s to 2003

On the ephemeral bubble

I WAS TWENTY-TWO years young when my journalism career began and fifty-four when it ended. By then, I had been a staff writer at three newspapers—four, technically, as the scrappy morning *Sentinel* was distinct from the singularly important *Milwaukee Journal* before they merged. But my education about working for a newspaper editor began in college.

Mizzou journalism students produce a city daily newspaper, *The Columbia Missourian*. In my senior year, I developed a crush on one of the *Missourian's* assistant editors, a stick-skinny graduate student with a disturbingly scraggly soul patch. My heart sank the afternoon he frowned as he returned to my mail slot a story I'd slammed together for the next day's paper, a magnificent account of a Boone County Rural Electrification Committee meeting. The meeting was a snorer, but I managed to energize my recap of it with a splashy assortment of adjectives and adverbs. There! I told myself. That'll grab the readers' attention.

Uh, no.

I waited a discreet four seconds before I retrieved the rejected story from my mailbox, for I was eager to know why my debut attempt at experimental journalism hadn't advanced to the copy desk. Up and down the margins of the story, the skinny assistant editor had written endearments to me. Oh, happy day! Doe-eyed and fluttery, I carried the story across the newsroom to his desk.

"You wrote KISS here," I said. "Did you mean it?"

His lifted his gaze from the hatchet-job he was completing on a classmate's story. "Yes," he said. "It means keep it simple, stupid."

The *Hannibal Courier-Post* was not a huge operation. A single news editor and one sports editor ran the show. For the first eight months of my journalism career, I worked for an affable news editor; Charlie's budget was tight but his patience with a cub reporter was boundless.

The *St. Louis Globe-Democrat* was an adjustment. I started out on the copy desk; my shift began in the early afternoon and lasted until ten or eleven at night.

One afternoon in the summer of 1972, word of a big story sizzled through the newsroom. Missouri Senator Thomas Eagleton withdrew his name after only eighteen days on the presidential ticket of Democratic candidate George McGovern when word leaked out that twelve years earlier Eagleton had been hospitalized for depression and had undergone electroshock therapy.

This was huge news in St. Louis. A junior editor handed me the story to edit and top with a headline. The piece would occupy most of the front page under an enormous 72-point, two-line headline that spanned all eight columns.

Alas, that headline was a problem. The larger the font size, the fewer letters fit on a page. For long minutes, I scribbled and scratched, counting each letter and space in my head, rearranging words, trying to find something that fit. But with key words like Eagleton, Vice-Presidential, McGovern, and Candidacy, the job was almost impossible.

The bulldog edition deadline came and went.

I sensed people standing right behind me. It was the *Globe* city editor, news editor, and the paper's silver-haired publisher. My stomach twisted. The men fidgeted a few more minutes, until finally the publisher reached over my shoulder and grabbed the pencil from my hand. Thoroughly mortified, I watched him quickly circle one of my works-in-progress and hand the scrap of paper to the copy desk chief. Loathe to question the publisher's choice, the copy chief rolled up the note paper without a glance at the selected headline. She shoved it into a canister and inserted the canister into a pneumatic tube. With a whoosh of air, my headline raced beneath the streets of St. Louis to the pressroom in the basement of the *Post-Dispatch* that served both papers.

The editors dispersed. I departed with my copy desk friends to the Press Club, where I ordered my usual dinner—warm rice pudding and a bourbon Old-Fashioned.

When we returned, the city editor was waiting beside a chair he had dragged to the center of the newsroom. "Underhill!" he called out. "Get over here!"

A hush replaced the usual clatter and din. I approached slowly and stopped ten feet from the chair. The city editor was a small man, and he was usually self-contained. But not this night. He beckoned to me, a wordless command to advance. I took another three steps. By now he was fuming. With a jerk, he repositioned the chair and indicated I should stand on it.

I considered my options. I could cry. I could tell him off and then quit. I could stand on the blasted chair.

I stood on the chair.

In the thundering silence, someone dropped a pencil. It sounded like an I-beam dropped from a crane. Typewriters fell silent. Ringing phones went unanswered. I held my breath.

"I have never," the City Editor began, loud enough to be heard out on the street, "never, EVER had to stop the presses, until tonight."

That established, he handed me a copy of the aborted first edition, one that would not reach a single doorstep or newsstand.

"Read what you wrote," he ordered. "Make it loud and clear."

I glanced at the fat, black headline marching across the page. What was the problem? In fact, given the colossal font and long words, I was amazed that I had produced something remotely coherent.

But what did I know? I was barely twenty-three years old at the time, closely parented and schooled in the main by nuns and Jesuits through my formative years. Under intense pressure to complete a headline, I had unknowingly created an appalling example of double entendre that went undetected until one of the press operators, doubled over with glee, phoned the *Globe* newsroom.

I read the headline.

"Louder," the City Editor barked.

I drew in a deep breath and shouted:

EAGLETON WITHDRAWS
FROM NO. 2 POSITION

Over gales of laughter that seemed to wash across the newsroom forever, a knucklehead on rewrite called out, "Hey Underhill, what exactly *is* the Number Two Position?"

I suffered greatly but not long. A metro daily newsroom exists on the ephemeral bubble of incessant deadlines. Typewriters resumed their clackety-clack staccato, telephones rang and were answered, the AP and UPI wires churned out the news of the world line by line that fell to the floor in paper coils, and my mortifying moment on the chair passed.

Today, such a thing would not happen without severe repercussions for the editor. But even back then, even a young woman schooled by nuns and closely parented knew that a setback could bring fresh opportunities.

There might or might not be a thread from that awful headline to the end of my duties on the copy desk. More likely, the transfer to a feature writing job a month later occurred because my second freelance story had turned up on the cover of *St. Louisan Magazine*.

In Milwaukee, I worked for all manner of editors. One of them, a deeply troubled woman who detected the recurring scent of her dead grandmother and who was bothered by visions of bees swarming her laundry basket, was carried off by orderlies after a late-night intervention at which I was present. Another editor had a habit of making printouts of stories before they were published and returning them to the reporter impossibly jumbled. We theorized she had scissored into sections the paper copy of our stories, tossed the pieces in the air like playing cards, and rearranged them in whatever order she picked them up.

The editor I most respected was the man who admired my work enough to nominate it for a Pulitzer Prize. But over the years, I have felt particular admiration for two other editors. Both are fine journalists with well-honed management skills, and yet at a glance they are as different as can be. One dressed in navy blue skirted suits and black flats and wore her hair with full bangs and a thick braid that fell to the small of her back. The other was partial to ponchos, midi-skirts, and statement earrings. Bangle bracelets marched up her arm, wrist to elbow. And she was bald.

Globe-Democrat c. 1972

Chapter 28
Transgressions
July 2003

I am news

ON JULY 11, I drive downtown for a meeting at the *Journal Sentinel.* In the lobby, I meet the lawyer Dennis hired. He is an older man, pale and quiet. Although he has a solid reputation, my impression is that everything about him—the rumpled suit, the sagging features, and sloping shoulders—telegraphs defeat. That's okay. I *am* defeated.

Someone from Human Resources directs us to a windowless room off the lobby, four floors below the newsroom. The lawyer and I sit side-by-side at a long conference table flanked by simple chairs. Editors and corporate executives walk in and take seats on the opposite side of the table, facing us. They are prepared.

The senior editor speaks slowly but clearly. In the past, he has been a champion of my career. Today, he appears to me to be sorrowed but decisive. Resolved. He begins by saying the newspaper has examined my past work. He has a slender packet. I tune out the rest; I cannot bear to think about what I have done. I start to bury my face in my hands and realize I have forgotten to take off the sunglasses I wore when I drove downtown. I wonder if I should do so now, and then the thought glides away.

Gutted, I focus only on the fact that I have lost my job at the *Journal Sentinel* through my failures. Worse, far worse, I have ruined my reputation.

The meeting moves swiftly. The lawyer Dennis hired tries to interject. Previously, I had instructed the man to not contest or protest anything, but he assumes there will be negotiations. He's mistaken.

When the editors finish, they rise in unison and leave the room. A guy from Human Resources oversees the rest.

Afterward, I am news. Journalism ethics has become a hot topic; my name joins a growing list of disgraced journalists.

Days after the meeting, the attorney phones. He says a *Milwaukee Magazine* reporter has contacted him. He says the man is writing an article about me and wants to interview me. I tell the lawyer to decline all requests.

In October, *Milwaukee Magazine* publishes a lengthy article about my fall from grace.[14] A month later, it runs a second piece.[15] The magazine writer uses comments from unnamed sources. He attributes a rumor with "Word has it . . ." In the November story, he writes that I applied for the college teaching job and then failed to withdraw the application during the summer.

The truth is, I did not request the job at Mount Mary College. The department chair offered it to me, unsolicited, unexpected.

The magazine writer also claimed I did not apologize. I did. I apologized to the group of editors during the first meeting in the *Journal Sentinel* newsroom.

The magazine runs a sketch depicting me as nearly nude, using my hands to shield my private parts. Every word of the magazine stories, every inch of the crude illustration, is a scalpel debriding ribbons of my flesh.

Through fall and early winter, articles, columns, essays, and analysis pieces about me appear elsewhere; some parrot the *Milwaukee Magazine* articles, freshened with additional thoughts and conjecture by the magazine writer. I have time to read about myself—the college has terminated me—but I don't.

I begin to second-guess my decision to remain silent, and I contact the Poynter Institute in Florida, the seminal resource for journalists. I summarize what happened. I tell the Poynter expert that there is a human factor here that was not part of the dialogue. He listens carefully. Then, in words that resonate with compassion, he advises me to remain silent. It will be seen as excuse-making if you try to explain, he says, and it won't go well for you.

I take him at his word.

Chapter 29
Onward, Somehow

Late summer 2003

There is a hole in my world

I AM NOT a saint. I do not cast myself as one. I have failed in ways large and small. In those cases, I have accepted the consequences without undue expectations.

Expectations are different from hopes, although the two sometimes intersect. An expectation is the belief that a thing will happen. Hope is not easily defined. It is fingertips ruffled across piano keys the night before an audition. Glowing votives in a dark church. Dandelion puffs blown into the air.

I have no expectation it will be so, but I hope that future assessments of my professional life will be balanced. I hope they are not based solely on my finest achievements or my most ignominious failures, but on the aggregation of every day's endeavors. I hope my legacy as a person will be framed not by those who judged me, but by those who knew me.

After fourteen years at the *Sentinel* and the *Journal Sentinel,* my job is over. My journalism career is over.

There is a hole in my world, and I am lost in it. Dennis showers me with optimism. Friends call. Want to go for coffee? Lunch? Wine? Anything?

Not yet.

I sequester at home by choice. I cannot bear to be with people from the newsroom, especially those who offer kind words of support because they don't believe I could have done what I did.

I am without hope again, and with that, the dangers of despair await. Eventually, the three women I love most redirect my dark thoughts. My mother, whose crises crackle over the Internet and demand my attention. And my daughters, whose problems seem almost humorous in contrast to mine and my mother's. With brimming eyes, I pull myself up, envisioning them as successful career women, brides, and mothers.

In late summer, Dennis and I drive Meg and everything she owns to St. Louis for the start of medical school. It is refreshing to be on the road. Milwaukee feels toxic to me.

After a final assurance from Meg that she doesn't need a thing, she'll be all right, and it's okay to go now, Dennis and I drive out to Thornhill, where yet another surprise awaits: An infestation of termites. Also, brown recluse spiders.

After another few days at the Marriott and a full-house fumigation, Dennis backs the car down Thornhill's long driveway, and we head for our home. Every mile takes me farther from the city I love and closer to the city that has lost faith in me.

> Pam – Hi Catherine. I hope you're enjoying your newfound leisure time. I haven't seen Mom since the latter part of April and, thus, my thinking may be altered after my upcoming visit. But I think Mom should continue to live at home for as long as she can and wishes to do so. In my judgment, she is still physically and mentally reasonably able to do so, with full-time assistance. I think we should respect her wishes. I would say that we see things a little differently regarding Mom's care. Also, I am sure that there are issues on which we agree. Certainly, we all want Mom's well-being. Luv, Pam.

> Catherine – Pam, out of love, concern, and devotion to our mother, I disagree with nearly every one of your points.

> Meg – Hi Mom and Dad. We dissected the lungs in Anatomy today, which was fantastic. Yay for sending free food. Luv, Meg

Soon, Underhill issues on top of my traumatic ouster from the ranks of working journalists are fueling the return of symptoms I thought I had overcome. I startle at sudden sounds during the day. I awake and roam the house at night. I sit on the couch and stare out the windows at home by myself, inert, tasked with few responsibilities except putting dinner on the table. I cannot say whether the spells last a minute half an hour. I really don't care. I have nowhere to go, no one to see, nothing productive to do, nothing to achieve.

Michele sends a strongly worded email. She tells me that I am withdrawing from the very people who can help pull me out of misery. She says it's a mistake to assume my professional future is bleak. She says everyone has faults and failings. She assures me that our friendship will not dissolve. She reminds me that she, too, has been at low points in the past and that I have stayed at her side. She assures me that we will get through this and that I will be the stronger for it.

> Catherine to Michele – Okay, how's Saturday for coffee? I
> promise to cry only once, with darn good cause.

Dr. Donna suggests I focus my energies on redirecting my future. I enroll in French language lessons. I set up a wardrobe planning program at a transitional home for young women who have aged out of the foster care system. My talks are aimed at helping them make good choices when they go on job interviews. On the bright side, I am available to visit Mother, Meg, and Claire, and free to explore other types of writing.

Meg and Claire phone frequently. Meg recently reported she received her first pair of bone cutters! Claire called to ask for her Christmas present. I remind her it is September. She explains that she needs funds for an overdue car insurance payment. Upon closely questioning her, Dennis and I learn that during the 24 hours Claire has been uninsured, she rear-ended a Mercedes.

Dennis is considering taking the Illinois bar exam.

> Catherine – Meg, thank you, dearest, for your thoughtful note.
> Yesterday, I observed a moment of silence for the heroes,
> victims, and families of the 9/11 attacks. Do you know what the
> best part is? Today's September TWELFTH!

> Ken – Hi doll. Pam called last night around suppertime.
> Agitated. Mom had stomach cramps all afternoon. Pam said
> she needs to leave early this morning. She's afraid Hurricane
> Isabel might suddenly make a miraculous leap into her flight
> path back to Ithaca. Pam is also "pissed" (her words) about the
> tacky furniture in the upstairs front blue bedroom the caregivers
> use. She would like me to order new furniture. And get the
> shower fixed.

I call Tom.

"How many showers do they need over there?" he says.

The following day, Ken sends an urgent email. Pam has left for Ithaca. Mom is in the hospital, diagnosed with C. difficile Colitis.

So, after an absence of half of a year, my sister finally made it to St. Louis, stayed a few days, watched her mother grow sicker and sicker, and left. And for the record, Hurricane Isabel made landfall as a Category 2 storm on the outer banks of North Carolina, which is nowhere near Ithaca, New York.

> Meg – Mom! You can tell people I was quite adept at tying off
> the rectum of our cadaver before we removed the GI tract, but
> that might not go over well in casual conversation.

Back in St. Louis for the seventh time since my father's funeral, I start cleaning out two of the bedrooms. Apparently, my mother regards the detritus of her children's school days as museum artifacts. I don't. Out go copies of Vatican encyclicals, three books by Berton, and stacks of outdated research on the Ovulation Method of Natural Family Planning. I stick Matt's ancient trophies in a box in the basement and give a wobbly metal desk to LaVerne, who wants it. And I write to my brothers and sister, their mother would like the orange bedroom repainted because the new color (which she chose) is too popsicle-y. Also, Mom would like a new rug for the yellow bedroom.

I'm going to need to come back soon. Mom's on a roll.

In late November, Ken writes that Tatiana is back from Ukraine, and she wants to work at Thornhill again. Thus begins anew my crusade to save my mother from the perils of an inappropriate caregiver.

I tell my siblings that Mom has difficulty understanding Tatiana's broken English. I remind them the ability to communicate clearly in a crisis and relay medical instructions to the family is essential. I describe how Mother wept when Tatiana showed her "home movies" of pitiful orphanages in Ukraine. I underscore there could be only one motive to manipulate a wealthy, vulnerable widow with that video. I remind my siblings that Tatiana took Mother to a house or apartment, sat her on a sofa, and then vanished into a bedroom with a man. I remind them that Tatiana fired our cleaning crew and hired her friend to clean at Thornhill.

Tatiana is pretty, tall and leggy, and congenial in temperament. Despite the woman's flaws, Mom likes her, which is all that matters to the only brother of mine who counts.

Cue another skirmish in the war of words in which opposing positions are stretched to ridiculousness.

The orphan movie? A positive experience. Broadened Mom's outlook on the world.

Right. Next up, a tour of Gitmo.

The field trip? The man probably was one of Tatiana's friends.

Ha! Really?

The most critical aspect is that Mom gets along well with Tatiana.

Wrong. Mom should have the final choice about the caregivers with her, but should choose from a list her adult children pre-approve.

Pam says we should all be proud of helping Mom through her grief and pain, restoring her home to good order, and finding a way for her to stay there with supervised care.

Sensing a stalemate, I point out that my brothers were pleased to interview and hire (or to hire without bothering to interview) the following:

A widow with a two-hour commute each way who quit before she even started.

A woman who collapsed and nearly died a week into the job.

A woman who lacked a driver's license.

An obese nursing student who required three energetic tries before successfully hoisting herself off the sofa.

A squeaky-voiced applicant looking forward to her twentieth birthday, which she will not observe for several years.

And Tatiana, whose command of the English language is littered with Ukrainian, Russian, and Polish.

Paul says he doesn't waste his time worrying about potential crises. I tell him that's okay; family members who are more preventatively inclined will step up.

He says that Jan, a nurse who works for C&C, should supervise Mom's meds. I point out that Jan quit a month ago.

Ken says he does not intend to consult Mother about Tatiana because he will not override my strong recommendations.

Afterward, Mother tells me that Tatiana phones Thornhill daily and has rung the doorbell three times seeking to be reinstated, even if it means firing someone else. Tatiana also apparently told our mother that her prior clients gave her expensive gifts and took her on their luxury vacations.

I write to my siblings: "Our sweet mother's concern is that she has nothing to give to Tatiana."

> Pam – Hello everyone. As a couple of you already know, I didn't make it to St. Louis last weekend as planned. I hurt my shoulder during aerobics.

Chapter 30
Compelling Reasons
2004

Both of them are pickled

CLAIRE AND I take Mom on a mini-vacation. For four days, we wallow in luxury on the club level of the Amelia Island Ritz-Carlton Hotel. Mom spends most of the time in the concierge lounge, where light meals and adult beverages are complementary. She begins each day with a hot breakfast and a chilled Bloody Mary and then moves on seamlessly to a champagne brunch, lunch with wine, a mid-afternoon snack with more wine, early cocktails, supper with wine, assorted desserts, and cordials. Claire paces her glass for glass. Both of them are pickled the entire time.

Soon, we careen into another family crisis.

Should I have known the deepening magnitude of my sister's illness? Yes and no. I've been juggling a few balls. Pam lives a thousand miles from me. And for weeks, she has been sending cheery emails about her son's upcoming wedding in Cincinnati.

On the weekend of the ceremony, I share a hotel room with Mother. Pam's room is two doors from ours. Matt and Tom are down the hall.

Shortly before the rehearsal dinner, Pam phones. Can I come to her room? Now?

She is waiting for me in the hall. The moment I see her, I freeze. On one side of her head, curlers angle off in odd directions. On the other side, her hair hangs limp. On the right side of her face, she has slathered thick layers of garish makeup. The left side of her face is bare. She is wearing a thin robe, nothing else.

The robe is gaping, and she's sobbing.

I back my sister into her room with soothing words. I have no idea what's wrong, and her explanations make no sense, but I repair her hair and makeup and help her into the lovely dress she has bought. Eventually, she calms.

The rehearsal dinner is in a private dining room at the hotel. Pam is seated at a table with her Underhill relatives. I am on one side of her, and Matt is on the other. By the time the salad arrives, Pam is trembling so violently the food falls away from her fork. Tears begin to stream down her cheeks. She starts to mumble. I have a real concern that if Pam takes one bite, she'll throw up. Matt and I make eye contact. We are both thinking the same thing: This is the Underhills' problem.

Pam starts to slip off her chair. Matt and I quickly rise. Supporting our sister in our arms, we half-walk, half-carry her from the room. No one else stirs.

I glance back at my nephew, the groom. His broad shoulders are slumped, his eyes filled with pain. He bravely forges on, for his bride, for the rest of his family, and their closest friends, but for him, it is a celebration drenched in misery.

Upstairs, Matt and I try to convince Pam to stay for tomorrow's church wedding, but she is in full-on torment. The hotel windows don't open. She cannot stay. She has to leave, has to get out, has to go immediately, go home to Ithaca, nobody will miss her, she's not essential, if she stays, she'll ruin it for everyone. On and on.

At midnight, we give up. A friend of the groom lives nearby. He and his wife have a guest bedroom. Pam is welcome to sleep there. Elise, Pam's daughter, makes the arrangements. David, Pam's younger son, waits in the hotel hallway, his face creased with worry and fatigue. David lives and works in New Zealand. He has flown halfway across the world to be at his brother's wedding. Now, he is crestfallen to see his mother's condition.

During the night, Elise and I agree that she and her mother will fly to Ithaca together immediately after the wedding. Elise will stay in Ithaca long enough to ensure that her mother gets psychiatric care.

Then, early the following morning, the wedding morning, the friend phones. Pam has vanished.

I realize what happened. In the dark of night, my fretful sister paced the guest room, consumed with paranoia, unfocused anger, and phobias she could not conquer or even describe. Finally, she called an airline reservation agent. At dawn, under a sky streaked with pastels, she tiptoed from the house to the waiting cab.

Even as her son is dressing for his wedding, his mother is walking down a concourse, ticket in hand, bound for Ithaca.

The wedding is bittersweet. At the altar, the groom weeps.

I blame everyone I can think of for not realizing how desperately ill Pam is. I blame myself for breaking a solemn promise.

My parents understood how vulnerable their daughter was; years ago, they asked me to be a helpmate to her throughout our lives. I promised I would, but it was tough. Pam was confrontational and unreliable. She backed out of trips at the last minute. She promised repeatedly to come to Thornhill, then canceled at the last minute. Mom would plunge into a decline, and I would put my life on hold to fill the void.

Instead of identifying why Pam would do such a thing so often, I focus on shoring up our mother. Instead of feeling compassion for my sister, I simmer with resentment. Instead of realizing she is incapable of being responsible, I continue to expect it from her.

And yet, how to stop loving a sister?

Days after the wedding, I write to Pam. I encourage her to begin the healing process with close medical and psychiatric guidance. Think of those who love you, I write.

Words come quickly to me. I know that my sister is disturbed. The truth is, I have no reason to believe she will—or can—commit to close, ongoing medical and psychiatric guidance. Elise flew to New York right after the wedding, but in a matter of days, she has to leave Ithaca and fly back to her own home and family. Then no one will be with Pam.

I do not step in. I do not step up. I default to her children. I tell myself they're responsible adults, but I sorely underestimate the damage to them that their mother's illness and broken marriage inflicted. I pray they are not as burned out as I am.

I do nothing. Maybe I've conquered one syndrome of PTSD. Perhaps I can finally walk away from that telephone kiosk on that New York corner that Dr. Donna keeps asking about. Maybe I can leave behind the urge to save everyone I think needs saving.

Maybe not.

After the wedding, Paul and I continue to tangle. It has come to define the current state of our relationship. This time, we disagree about the validity of documents our parents drew up that authorize Pam and me to oversee the process by which their personal property (household effects) would eventually be distributed among the family.

I stew awhile and then resume fine-tuning the components of a meaningful post-journalist life. I start volunteering at a school for Hispanic girls. I continue my weekly wardrobe planning sessions with the young women in the group home. Dr. Donna wants me to work on a memoir about 9/11. I might or might not get to that.

Pam writes. She's planting flowers and looking forward to summer houseguests. My sister has always been a writer of smoothly deceptive notes.

Elise writes, too. She's worried. Her mother seems fine one minute and gets worked up over the littlest thing the next minute. She has not been going to treatment sessions. She's canceled all visitors.

I fly back to St. Louis, where Meg's love-life issues are a welcome diversion. A friend wants to fix her up with a date. The friend has pictures of a few prospects.

"Mom, they're massive, and they're rather scary looking," Meg tells me. "One guy is a computer hacker. And there's the photo of all six of them in camouflage-wear with giant rifle-type guns and bright orange hats, surrounded by a bunch of pick-up trucks."

Paul writes again. He finds Mom's history of passing down pieces from her jewelry collection to Pam and me over the years unorthodox and disturbing.

The written word functions quite well as a sword, and so Paul and I proceed to lunge, attack, feint, parry, riposte, and counter-attack with words.

Paul says he does not mistrust me and regrets that I think that. He acknowledges, however, that he and I rarely agree. He says he intentionally backs away from participating in dysfunctional family shit (his word). He says one of his goals is to keep his mother safe from the hasty and emotion-laden judgments of one of her children. He says he thinks I am emotional. He suggests I write a book.

He says he has had three glasses of wine.

No. Really?

I write that I will countenance no interference in my relationship with my mother. I write that the value of the jewelry given to Pam and me over the years is minuscule when cast against the value of Mother's assets currently being managed by Paul, Tom, and Matt, and that in such matters, my brothers have my unquestioning confidence.

Touché, I tell myself.

Chapter 31
What Really Matters
Autumn 2004

Only in desperation

UNDERHILL ISSUES ARE swirling, and still we are as divided as ever.

Ken's wife contacts me. Tina says Ken is going through a major midlife crisis. He wants the excitement of his bachelor days. He has lost interest in his family. He moved out of their house and is sleeping in his old bedroom at Thornhill. Tina suspects his drug use is habitual. She has found cocaine paraphernalia in their home and discovered their young son playfully mimicking his father's cocaine use at the kitchen table. Recently, Ken almost slugged a guy he didn't even know.

Ken? Ken jokes. He doesn't fight. What's going on down there?

Ken writes. He is afraid his marital problems have caused Mom's shingles. He asks for a $2,500 loan from Mom's accounts. He has his eye on an apartment in a trendy historic area of the city.

Paul's reply reveals his capacity for empathy, generosity, and human decency.

He tells Ken he is genuinely sorry about the breakup of his marriage. He assures Ken that every marriage has its problems, and he knows Ken and Tina will do what is best for their children. He says he thinks Ken is in the worst stage of the breakup and that things will be better in the future. He says he is confident that Mother will understand eventually. He says Ken's problems certainly did not give Mom shingles.

Paul goes on to say that if $2,500 is what Ken estimates he will need, then the amount should be doubled. He says angst over money should not consume Ken at this time. He says a direct infusion of cash to Ken now should not be regarded as a loan and that there will be no interest assessed, no formal papers drawn up, and no need to worry about paying it back.

He closes by telling Ken that the money part is easy and advises Ken to worry about what matters.

It is one of the most beautiful letters I have ever read.

During the ragged remains of 2004, Underhill issues weigh on me. The urge to solve them, to *be there*, to keep everyone I love safe siphons the attention Dennis and our daughters deserve. I lose focus on rebuilding a meaningful life, stop mentoring at the group home, and decline requests to volunteer more often at the middle school.

In September, as usual, the nightmares return. Also, the exaggerated startle stuff. I know to expect it. I make plans to return to St. Louis. It's time I checked on Mom's caregivers, her medications, the house and yard. I need to make sure the lancets are gone. I need to check her fingertips for fresh blood. I need to be certain she's safe. That's the only way I can be sure I will never again walk out the front door at Thornhill and leave my mother weeping in the foyer.

Paul and Matt have been to St. Louis before me this time. They meet with Ken and try to convince him to enter in-patient treatment for drug addiction. For once, I stay on the sidelines of a rescue.

The sibling intervention fails. Tina is devastated.

In an email, I reassure Ken that we love him, and we will never stop.

Ken moves to the apartment in the city. Ken fails a drug test. Ken loses his job.

Pam questions why Tina didn't come to us with her suspicions long ago. She says if living with Tina exacerbated Ken's need for relief in the form of occasional cocaine use, then at least he's free of "that problem." She says Tina needs to face the music and find full-time employment.

I go ballistic. It's not surprising. It's September. I'm edgy, short-tempered, and exhausted. I startle at minor unexpected noises. I turn off television clips about the World Trade Center attacks. I wake from awful dreams and roam the house, reliving the North Tower collapse.

I don't have to search anymore for the reason I'm always a mess in September. I know it's the lingering effect of trauma, a triggered response to something I wrongly assumed I had conquered.

I tell Pam I'm in no position to predict how a woman like Tina, a naïve, reverent, sweet-natured suburban wife and mother would react when she discovers two throw-away wine glasses in the gym bag her absentee husband carries to his young son's ball games, and when, bit by horrifying bit, she realizes he is addicted to street drugs. But when these and other heartbreaking discoveries creep up on a woman who for more than sixteen years has known her husband to be quirky but who has believed him to be true, I can imagine the reaction is initially numb denial. Then pleading. Then arguments and ultimatums. Only then would she approach his siblings for help. Only in desperation.

I end with a zinger: We assumed we know Ken better than his wife. We do not. We have merely known him longer.

Matt tries to soothe me. He says some family members stay on the sidelines and participate in the family discourse only when they have a gripe, but I have been involved at every turn, possibly more involved than I should be, but that's the way I am, he says. Big-hearted. Glass never half-empty. He says we will all get through these trials with the grace of God.

Matt doesn't know that Pam has been venting to me for years, endless diatribes on a lifetime of family topics she views through a skewed prism. He doesn't realize how often I shoved to the background my husband, my growing daughters, feature stories I was working on, even dinners in the oven when calls from my sister devolved into sharp-edged harangues that left me drained and disheartened.

Matt doesn't know that Mom and Dad asked me to promise to be Pam's family connection and confidante.

My family has characterized me and my sister in degrees of contrast all my life. She is fretful, and I am forceful. She is insecure. I am confident. She is emotionally fragile. I am a pillar of strength. They see this as an admirable quality, but it can be a millstone that grinds with the weight of obligations and expectations I now need to shed.

My family has no idea of the toll being "the strong one" exacts. I have not shared with them that interceding during the abuse to Mom in the den traumatized me. I've not told them that I fell into a depression so profound that I considered ending my life.

None of the Underhills have asked me to describe what it was like to be in New York on 9/11, so they have little basis for understanding the trauma I experienced at the time or its residual symptoms. I do not think they know the details of how my journalism career ended in public humiliation, and why. Based on casual remarks over the years, I have the impression my siblings regarded my work as a hobby and the income as "pin money." We did not exactly grow up in an enlightened household.

They do not know about the promise our parents extracted from me long ago, and that it's drowning me in frustration and resentment. They assume my hyper-attention to Mother is motivated by a desire to exert control over her, a power play by "the strong one."

They really have no idea.

I am so furious about Pam's sanctimonious email that I fail to consider my sister from her perspective. It does not occur to me that she might yearn to travel, to return to her childhood home, and stay awhile with the mother she emulated years ago. I do not consider that Pam might be mortified after backing out of trips and be genuinely sorry for the wreckage when she does so.

I have hardened my heart. I tell myself I couldn't care less if she is miserable.

It's a lie.

Chapter 32
Anxieties

Late Autumn 2004

Do not lose faith in yourself

MOTHER BROKE HER leg getting out of bed. Now she needs a portable walker, a leg brace, a chairlift for the stairs, and a walk-in shower and grab bars.

Pam pumps out chipper emails that acknowledge the efforts Tom and I have made for Mother. She apologizes for questioning our judgment.

Tina files for divorce.

Meg is having trouble getting to sleep and staying asleep.

> Catherine – Dearest Meg, you were born to be a physician. You will move past the obstacles, and your father and mother will do whatever it takes to assist you. We have only one condition: that you not lose faith in yourself.

Chapter 33
Spider Webs
2005

Thinking about writing something

CLAIRE IS FINISHING graduate school at DePaul University. Soon, she will be qualified to teach English, speech, and drama classes. She has taken to conversing about the paradoxes of the Age of Enlightenment.

Our daughters have vacationed in Puerto Rico, Salzburg, Prague, and Dublin this year. Dennis and I wonder if the rigorous gestalt of graduate school is one long holiday.

I am taking French lessons again, serving on the Hidden Reserve Condo Association board, volunteering at the middle school, seeing Dr. Donna less frequently, and thinking about writing again.

The Underhills schedule a family meeting for January in St. Louis. On the eve of the meeting, Pam writes to say she cannot be with us.

Paul sits down across from Mother and indicates a chair off to the side for me. He tells her he is not pleased about the letter she wrote stating that Pam and I are to oversee the dispersal of the household items among her heirs. He says he'll have to deal with that. I am still stewing when he turns to the issue of her jewelry.

"I want my jewelry to go to my daughters," Mom says, twice.

It would appear that Paul has hit a brick wall. He has not. He suggests his mother make an appointment with an attorney and compile a new list that describes each piece of her jewelry, its appraised value, and whom she wants to inherit it.

All three of us know that will not happen.

Our mother is in a wheelchair. She requires constant supplemental oxygen. She takes prescription medicine to lessen pain. She cannot bathe herself unassisted. She cannot drive. She cannot negotiate a staircase. She is oblivious to her financial position. She needs to be diapered.

The following day, we gather in the living room. A life-size oil painting of St. Matthew hangs on the wall behind the long sofa and above the loveseat is a painting of a French farmhouse. Near the fireplace, two chairs face the marble chessboard Mom and Dad bought in Italy years ago. On the drum table sits a bible inscribed with generations of births. My old sheet music is still in the piano bench.

Thornhill is a house imbued with things of meaning, if only to us.

My brothers discuss our mother's will, her assets, her tax situation. Afterward, Paul suggests that because I live out of town, someone other than me should serve as Mother's medical power of attorney. Seeing no support from the crowd, he drops the matter. The meeting grinds on about financial issues, household maintenance, remodeling.

I stay on at Thornhill a while after everyone leaves. One day, I wake up to excruciating pain. I drive myself to St. John's Mercy Hospital, pass a kidney stone, return to Thornhill, and take mother out for a manicure.

Apprehension, anxiety, fear, moodiness, broken sleep, agitated dreams, and exaggerated startle reflex are part and parcel of PTSD. I have been dealing with these symptoms for four years. In the coming months, I make more trips to Thornhill, take more phone calls from Pam, worry about Ken, worry about Mother, worry and worry about my daughters, who are fine. The adverse impact on my health was probably inevitable.

I've heard that people who have come close to death are aware ever afterward that that they have been gifted with "extra time." So they treasure each day and try to use the gift of extra time well.

I understand that. I'm acutely aware of striding into peril on 9/11 and staggering away unharmed, physically at least. I think about how lucky I am all the time, undoubtedly too much. I'm thankful beyond measure for the extra time I have to live out my natural life alongside my husband, and to be here with my daughters well into their maturity.

But I have changed fundamentally ever since I witnessed the horror of the World Trade Center attacks. I changed when I watched the impact zones pour out greasy black smoke, and when I saw lost souls at the windows jump to certain death. I changed when I crouched behind a mail bin, praying it would shield me from the concussive blast of a collapsing 110-story skyscraper. I changed when I realized that had I only asked more questions before giving a thumbs-up to firefighters on a red truck, they would not have died twelve minutes later. They would have lived to return to wives, fathers, sisters, neighbors. To Mikey.

Being so close to the violent end of my life has left me ever on the lookout for unexpected danger. I suspect it everywhere, all the time, convinced that a kind of harm I can't quite define might be waiting around the next corner, speeding the wrong way through the intersection up ahead, lurking on the far side of the door, falling out of the sky. But if I am vigilant, if I'm ready, then maybe I can prevent another tragedy. And so I live the gift of extra time ever on alert.

It drives Dennis and our daughters nuts. They don't understand that people could die if I'm not careful. People did die. Heroes on a red truck died.

Finally, good news. In fact, news good enough to substantially ease my worries. A big-busted, big-hearted, Baptist choir singer named Shirley has climbed aboard the carousel of caregivers at Thornhill. She joins sweet, soft-spoken, efficient LaVerne as the best of the best. Our prayers are answered.

By now, Mom's bones are brittle as pond ice. In early June, she breaks a hip. No one knows how it happened. No one is surprised. After a brief hospital stay, she is transferred to Suncrest, a rehabilitation center fifteen minutes west of Thornhill.

Paul flies to St. Louis. He reports that Mom is in rough shape, in substantial pain and exhausted from chronic diarrhea. She will need to be at Suncrest for weeks. Before he leaves, he directs the staff to move his mother to a private room.

LaVerne and Shirley are on it. They now are working their shifts at Suncrest. When they notice that Suncrest combines the laundry of its patients, they take our mother's things back to Thornhill and wash them there.

Paul is still adamant that Mother return to Thornhill as soon as she is able, to live out her life there.

I tell my sister and brothers that everything I have done for our mother has maintained or corrected her health, stabilized her care, and elevated her spirits. I remind them that Mom has had three bone fractures in the past year, and if there is a fourth, if it is due to a situation at Thornhill, I will come down strong on a transfer to a senior care facility.

In June, Mom is diagnosed with congestive heart failure. Even more devastating, we learn that she has developed pulmonary fibrosis, a progressive scarring of the lungs' interior that makes it increasingly difficult to breathe. There is no cure.

I fly back to St. Louis.

After Mom has had a good night's sleep and a good breakfast, and after a couple of games of morning Scrabble I make sure to lose, I drive her to see the pulmonologist. The news is terrible. The netting of thread-like scars on her lungs is advanced. She will need supplemental oxygen day and night for the rest of her life.

Pam has promised to come to Thornhill after I leave. When the date of her arrival nears, Mom and the caregivers lay in extra food and plan meals. Shirley bakes a cake. On the morning of her arrival, Mom puts on a dress, has her hair fixed, applies lipstick, and waits and waits.

What a sorry mess.

In early autumn, Dennis and I take a vacation to Italy. On the last day of the trip, the desk attendant at the Hotel Farnese in Rome summons me for an international phone call. Standing in an old-fashioned wood and glass telephone booth just off the small lobby, I learn that my Uncle Jay Meier, my mother's only brother, has died unexpectedly. Heart attack, they think.

Dennis and I fly directly to St. Louis. Again, I find myself writing a eulogy on an airplane. At the service, I talk about all the happy occasions when Underhills celebrated holidays with Meiers, about the blinding light of Uncle Jay's movie camera, and the way he laughed—eyes crinkled, nose raised, lips parted to reveal a complete set of teeth, head nodding in amusement.

When we drop our suitcases in the back hall at Thornhill, LaVerne tells us she's seen moths fluttering in closets.

"And Catherine," she says in a voice I would recognize to this day, "your mother's air conditioner's conked out again."

> Catherine – Siblings, our 82-year-old mother is wheelchair-bound, relies on constant supplemental oxygen to breathe without labor, and has been diagnosed with a chronic, worsening, incurable lung disease. She is prone to hypertension when even mildly anxious, and for the second time, she has had to sit at length in a dark house through a stormy afternoon. She tried to read her newspaper by flashlight. She did not know where she would sleep that night. Is this what you want?

> Catherine – Ken, if something happens in the house, show the EMTs her medical directive immediately, and phone me directly. You might have to be strong to fulfill your mother's trust in you. In the end, you and I have accepted a heavy responsibility.

Pam makes it to Thornhill. She stays four nights and fills her time with Mother marvelously. She drives Mom across the river to Belleville and the Our Lady of the Snows Shrine, which Mother loves. They visit the Missouri Botanical gardens, where the last autumn flowers are still in bloom. Finally, they stop at Resurrection Cemetery and lay flowers on Dad's grave. I admire the efforts Pam has made, and for a short while I am contented. Then, Shirley phones.

"Catherine, your mother's nighttime 'awake' caregiver been sleepin' on the job."

"Dozing?"

"Conked out."

"How long?"

"All night!"

Chapter 34
Thy Kingdom Come
2006

There is no magic medicine

FOR ALMOST THREE years, my mother has endured adversity without complaint. She has prevailed over polymyalgia rheumatica, giant cell arteritis, and temporary blindness. She has outlived her husband and moved past the desecration of her home. She lives with the degradation of her memory, recurrent depression, chronic pain. She has suffered spine surgery, broken bones, shingles, pneumonia, and bladder infections. Her bones are brittle. Her lungs require oxygen delivered from a canister. She needs a chair lift for the stairs and a wheelchair everywhere else. She shares her home with a cartwheel of caregivers. She takes prescribed medicines by the handful. She is diapered at night.

My mother has spent hours in hospital emergency rooms and weeks at Suncrest, a rehab center a few miles from Thornhill. She has been calm and accepting during power outages. Her elder daughter cancels visits. Her troubled son has moved back in with her.

She has pulmonary fibrosis. It will kill her.

My mother is indomitable. Almost.

On March 18, she marks her eighty-third birthday with a dinner at a nearby restaurant. Her recently widowed sister-in-law, one of her four sons, and one of her twelve grandchildren join her at the table. A pitiful turnout.

In late May, Shirley phones from Thornhill. Hornets are nesting between one of the bedroom windows and the screen.

Diane writes. Squirrels are eating the patio flowers.

Dennis and I leave the country and join two friends in London.

On June 8, Meg is at Barnes Hospital, assisting in the extraction of a teaspoon from a patient's stomach. Her grandmother is at St. John's Mercy Medical Center, ten miles west of Barnes, undergoing surgery to implant a cardiac pacemaker.

In July, the family is horrified to learn that the pacemaker model inserted into our mother's chest was recalled months ago. The batteries can drain too quickly. Patients could develop infections at the implant sites.

The surgeon's office asks if we would like to schedule Mrs. Underhill for a "pacemaker pulse generator change-out?"

In a rare moment of unity, we agree to decline the offer and fire the surgeon. We should sue, but none of us have the energy to do so.

In early August, Diane confides to me that my mother has been crying, which breaks my heart. I tell Diane to make sure the caregivers are comforting but also to give Mom her space. My mother has every right to cry. I would be concerned if she didn't.

Claire writes. She apologizes for being out of touch lately. She's been busy with rehearsals for a new show, the Dream Theatre Company production of *Ismene*. Claire has enormous talent. In the title role, she almost makes the company's radical new rendering of *Antigone* understandable. Almost.

> Catherine – It seems as if only weeks ago you were toddling around in a play group, coming home from kindergarten with a Crayola drawing, driving the minivan out to a party with your high school friends, graduating from college. Your childhood and youth have gone faster than Dad and I thought possible. Through it all, darling, we have been exceptionally proud of you and impressed by your accomplishments, your character, and all the enjoyable facets of your personality.
>
> Claire, we have watched you mature into a fine young woman who is at home in one of America's busiest cities. We have stood by and supported you as you pursued a degree in a field that uses your natural ability to connect with young people. Deciding to redirect your career path and having the fortitude to pursue it at the graduate-degree level will result in a life that is satisfying and rewarding. The finish line is in sight. We hope that your progress toward a teaching certificate and Master of Education degree will remain focused. Always, Mother

In September, Claire registers for the last of her classes at DePaul. Her academic advisor suggests she take "Understanding Poetry 401."

"Why?" Claire demands.

"It's mandatory."

Claire turns on her heel, dismissive. At the door, she tells the man, "Not mandatory for me. I already understand poetry!"

That's the Meier in my Claire.

Shirley phones. Mom's purse is stuck in a desk drawer. "And, Catherine, the coffee maker conked out."

Mom has another appointment with the pulmonologist. She is now constantly short of breath. After he orders a richer mix of supplemental oxygen, my sweet, foggy Mother asks the man when she will get better. He looks her in the eye.

"Merrilee," he says, "there's no magic medicine to make you well."

She was crushed.

That afternoon, Pam cancels another visit.

I remind my sister that our mother is eighty-three years old and chair bound. That she has outlived her husband, her only brother, and effectively her only sister suffers from dementia, in California. A misdiagnosed brain-cell disorder has left Mom with almost no short-term memory and with severely reduced practical functionality. The pieces of her right femur are held together with a foot-long steel rod and six bolts. She suffers from a permanent and degenerative lung disease that leaves her breathless if the oxygen tube is removed even briefly. Since Dad's death, she has undergone spine fusion surgery, has broken her leg and then shattered it. She suffers recurrent urinary infections because she must be diapered. Shingles has left her with nerve discomfort. She is medicated for depression. She has a damn defective appliance in her chest that might this very minute be leaking battery fluid.

I ask my sister to refrain from informing Mom or her caregivers about an upcoming visit until she pulls up the driveway at Thornhill.

In early November, Mom is back in St. John's. She is badly short of breath and her spine is crumbling. New fractures have left her in ghastly pain. The doctors suggest another kyphoplasty spine procedure, which we take to mean a second injection of the cement-like stuff that resulted in only marginal relief the first time. Meanwhile, to keep her spine from deteriorating further, hospital staffers fit her with a corset—a torment of stiff fabric and metal boning that she must wear it at all times, except when sleeping. And with that, our mother is conveyed back to Suncrest, the rehab place.

From Milwaukee, I phone Ken and ask him to drive out to Thornhill and bring the small oil painting of the house to Suncrest.

"And Ken, bring her favorite blanket, too, the white furry one."

Matt writes. He says he has plane tickets to see Mother in mid-December, almost six weeks from now. He says he can adjust his schedule depending on how Mom is doing. I tell him there is no way of knowing how Mom will be doing by dinnertime, much less by the middle of December.

The surgery will last two hours. It requires intubation and a respirator. Mom will be under general anesthesia, lying prone on her stomach.

We all agree to the procedure. It's the only hope to relieve the pain.

Pam sends me a note of thanks for being a strong advocate for our mother.

The procedure takes place November 30. Shortly thereafter, Mom is returned to Suncrest.

I have a ticket to fly to St. Louis on December 4. On December 3, Mother goes into a pulmonary crisis. An ambulance speeds her from Suncrest back to St. John's. Shirley follows the ambulance in Mother's car. On any other day, it might have been LaVerne, but LaVerne is home with a bad cold.

As soon as Shirley gets to the hospital, she dials my number.

"Come, Catherine," she shouts into the phone. "Come right now!"

I alert my sister and brothers and catch the first flight. That afternoon, I meet Tom and Ken in the hospital lobby. Their heads are bowed. They have shoved their hands deep into the pockets of their winter jackets. There's little to say. We take the elevator up and make our way to Mom's room.

Shirley's bulky frame spills over the seat of the bedside chair. She is holding Mother's hand and the contrast is profound. Shirley's hand is pudgy and dark, her thick fingers dimpled at the knuckles. Mother's are limp, the nails flat and ridged. Under papery skin bleached by pain to translucence, each long bone and wormy vein is distinct. Beneath a light blanket, her form is flat and unmoving except for the jagged spasms of her chest as she labors for air. Oxygen flows into a mask that covers her mouth and nose.

"Mom?" I whisper, and she opens her eyes. I smooth a wisp of hair from her forehead and bend to kiss her, lightly, for her skin is shiny as ironed tissue.

Shirley starts to rise, to give us space. I motion for her to stay. She is needed. Wanted. She settles again, casting her gaze to the window and beyond it to a leaden December sky, offering the dying mother, the heartsick daughter, a semblance of privacy.

Soon I must contact my three distant siblings. Although I have a considerable vocabulary, although I worked on and off for thirty years as a newspaper reporter and feature writer, a describer, a recorder of people and places, events and deeds, I struggle now for words to describe over the phone how it is here, watching our mother try to breathe.

I could tell them that her every gasping attempt to get air is a ragged, gravelly chuff that wracks her diminished body, and for hours she has endured it with silent grace and resignation. But I don't say that. What would be the point? I phoned them hours ago. They aren't coming.

Ken slips away. Tom and I stay on until in the early evening, he signals me. In the hall, he says we will need hot food and a night's sleep to fortify us for what is to come. We quibble about who will go and who will stay. Behind us, Shirley's frame fills the doorway.

"You two go," she says. "I'll stay."

I assume we will be back in an hour, so I agree. In the elevator, my thoughts are with my mother. I don't concern myself with how utterly spent Shirley must be, although dark smudges under her eyes tell the story. I don't calculate the hours Shirley has been on duty with my mother, although the arithmetic is easy.

Shirley, a paid-by-the-shift attendant employed by an agency hired by the Underhills, has kept vigil over our mother for two nights and three days. Now, she offers to stay with Mother a third night, prompted by the imminent desertion of the only two Underhills still in the hospital at nightfall. By the time Tom eases his car through the parking garage exit, I am drenched in guilt. Once again, I have walked out on someone in need, someone in crisis, someone I could have helped—saved. I resolve to go back as soon as I can.

At Tom's condominium, I wheel my suitcase to his spare bedroom. With no intention of doing so, I fall asleep immediately. At dawn, I see my phone on the pillow. Shirley has not called.

Tom is fixing breakfast. I ought to call a taxi, but I fear that it would take longer than waiting for Tom. Finally, he reaches for his car keys.

Mother is much worse. Yesterday each breath was a monumental struggle that shuddered her entire body. Today she is too exhausted for that level of effort. Her breathing is slower, weaker, shallower, and far less effective. Every tattered intake of air sounds as if it is sucked through a clogged straw and expelled through wet gravel. Her death is a ghastly, torturous, slow-motion drowning.

Shirley is humming, soft and low. She has not moved from the bedside chair. God love her.

I sit on the far side of the hospital bed. Mother is mildly sedated, in and out of consciousness. I whisper the words to the *Memorare*.

"Remember, oh most gracious Virgin Mary, that never was it known, that anyone who fled to thy protection, implored thy help, or sought thy intercession, was left unaided . . ."

Under the oxygen mask, Mother's lips form the words along with me. Together we petition the heavens.

I sing "The First Noel" and then "Silent Night." When my voice breaks, Shirley draws herself up. She starts "Amazing Grace," and her firm, clear voice swells into the hallway. She stretches the lyrics like taffy and gives each syllable a full measure of notes. The rich resonance of her voice infuses a place of pain and sadness with the balm of spiritual music. Under the sheet, Mother taps her toe to the lilting melody, and when she manages a weak smile, I turn my face to the window and weep for the pity of it.

Tom and Ken step into the room and stand at the foot of the bed awhile, then return to the hall to make phone calls, send messages, and wait.

For years, the three of us have worn ourselves to the bone in service to our failing mother. So many times, we have had to stand up to siblings who thought they knew better than we did. Now, during the final agony of our mother's life, we are too sorrowed to feel anything but the sadness of the moment.

I walk around the bed and rub Shirley's shoulders. I suggest she go home, get a hot meal, and sleep. I cannot think of a more selfless woman, one truer to her mission of service, one who more ardently lives her faith. If there are angels on Earth, Shirley is among them.

Alone in the room with Mother, I think about how we owe LaVerne Sanford and Shirley Gore. They met our mother's every whim and need with tenderness and compassion. They entertained her with light humor even as they shouldered heavy responsibility. Despite ice storms and power outages, blizzards and heat waves, endless doctor appointments, and extended trips to the emergency room, LaVerne and Shirley did not fail us. Worries over an ill, elderly parent never go away, but knowing our mother was safe in their care eased my mind.

My thoughts drift. In my mind, I see an afternoon from the past. I'm at Thornhill again. When LaVerne leaves in her car to buy groceries for our dinner, Mother tells me she'd like to give La Verne and Shirley each a gift to let them know they are valued. I suggest we start with LaVerne, and I suggest a small flowering tree for her yard. The next day, with the sapling in the trunk of Mom's car, we drive to a quiet residential street in north St. Louis County.

I park Mom's Lexus in front of LaVerne's house, a red brick ranch with a big picture window. A little girl in a pink dress is roller skating up the lane. Ribbons tied to her corn-row hairdo match her dress.

LaVerne answers the door. Her eyes grow wide as saucers. She hesitates a moment and then invites us in. "Please, sit," she begins before launching into a string of excuses about the state of things. The state of things is that her house is immaculate. I admire porcelain figurines in a curio cabinet and framed photos of her daughters on a wall. She fusses, straightens a lace doily on the back of a chair, offers sweet tea, brings out cookies.

"We have something for you," I tell her. "It's in the car."

As we rise to leave, LaVerne takes me aside.

"You and your mother," she whispers, peering at me through oversized glasses, "you're the first white people ever stepped inside this house."

At the hospital, nurses cycle in and out of the room, checking monitors and adjusting IV lines. Mother is breathing in quick, light puffs now. Her lips are blue. When she opens her eyes, I bend close.

"I just want it over," she gasps.

"I know, Mom. Soon."

I meet with Tom and Ken in the hall. We find a nurse and ask to talk with the doctor on call.

He is young, with a high forehead and a kind, focused gaze behind tortoiseshell glasses. He leads us to a conference room and closes the door.

I try to describe our mother's wretched, hopeless condition, her misery, *our* misery.

"You would like to take your mother to a different level of care," he says, part question, part statement. After each of us nods, he withdraws a pen from the pocket of his lab coat and writes a new medication order.

Meg arrives soon after we return to Mother's room. She hugs me and then runs her fingers lightly through her grandmother's hair. At the touch, Mom opens her eyes and motions for Meg to pull down the oxygen mask for a moment.

"How is Deepti?" Mom asks.

Meg's roommate, Deepti, had been sick with a cold. How beautiful that a dying woman remembers this little nugget from her granddaughter's life. Meg's features melt in an expression of compassion and sorrow. As a medical school student, she has witnessed the clinical process of dying during her hospital rotations, but I do not want her to see *this* death. I ask her to say a final goodbye.

After she leaves, I ask Mom if she wants to talk with Pam, Paul, and Matt. She nods.

I dial them one by one and hold the phone to Mom's ear. They tell her they love her. They tell her she has been a wonderful mother. They tell her she will soon be with Our Lord. They tell her goodbye. During each call, Mom signals me to remove the oxygen mask so that she can say a word or two. Afterward, she covers the receiver while she labors to catch her breath. In this last, selfless act, she spares her absent children from hearing the gruesome, guttural sounds of her struggle. The moment each call ends, she gulps for air, gets almost none, and goes into spasm. It bleeds my heart.

I regard the calls as a gift from me to my mother. Not to Pam, cloistered in Ithaca. Not to Paul, far from his father and now his mother when they were on their deathbeds. Not to Matt, praying in Yuma.

I tell Tom to find a nurse. It's past time for the second dose of the new medication, which I gather is a potent narcotic.

"I asked already," Tom says. "I don't think they'll do it."

Oh, yes, they will.

I march down the hall and buttonhole the nearest nurse. I make it clear we expect her to carry out the doctor's order. We walk in tandem to Mother's room. As soon as the nurse adjusts the IV line and tubes, the pace of the drip quickens.

A hospital counselor takes over Shirley's chair and launches into an explanation about what will happen afterward—the paperwork, the protocols, and hospital procedures. I interrupt.

"We want to take our mother back to Thornhill," I tell the woman. "We want her to be able to die at home, not here."

The woman frowns. It's a bad idea, she says. Your mother won't make it. She will die on a gurney in the hall, in the elevator, the lobby, or in the ambulance. Do you want that?

What I want is for this blasted counselor to go away. I turn to Mother and sing "Silent Night." When I get to the heavenly hosts, she breathes her last.

For a moment, I wonder if the essence of her is still there somehow, so I stay still. Eventually, I walk to the window. The December afternoon is mud-gray. In the waning of the day, clusters of bare-limbed trees and scattered houses stand out against the gloaming, for the homeowners have festooned branches, rooflines, and doors with red and green bulbs. One house, though, is different. In the front yard is a life-sized display of three figures outlined with white and yellow lights. I squint into the darkness. It's a trio of angels blowing golden horns.

> Meg – Mom, on this blustery, snowy night, I want to say that I remember my beautiful, graceful, kind, and courageous grandmother. Words can't express how I loved her and respected her, or the influence she had on the woman I've become. I see so much of her wonderful qualities—and what I loved about her—in you, as well, which keeps her alive for me every day. Miss you and love you dearly, Meg.

Outside Tom's condominium, the wind picks up. Icy gusts thrash the boughs of a balsam fir in the yard. Clouds heavy with moisture lumber into view from the west.

I dream first of angels with wings of glass silhouetted against a mottled moon and galaxies spinning away to places I cannot see, cannot be. Next, I dream of infant stars yet to bear names. Before my closed eyes, they gather and swirl like a murmuration of starlings, spangling the velvet sky.

During the ashy hour before dawn, I dream of an old star, a dying star on its final journey. With the last of its spirit, it speeds toward its diminishment, trailing a phosphorescent slipstream that showers the world below with sequins of gorgeousness.

I wake to the blue light of a December morning and breathe a clear spot on the frosty bedroom window. The season has delivered its first dusting of snow. Out on the lawn, tufts of brittle grass pierce the white scrim. Here and there across the undulating snowfield, flakes spark in the morning sun, as if from high above a mother's jewel box had opened and scattered the world with diamonds.

I take up a pen and begin another eulogy.

Eulogy for Mother
Merrilee Meier Underhill
1923 – 2006

A woman suited to graceful pastimes

THERE IS NO way to sum up a life in a few paragraphs, especially one as richly textured as our mother's, and no need to try. The threads of the whole cloth that was our mother's life are a tapestry woven over eight decades, a work of art as fine as ever there was.

Merrilee Meier was a child of privilege, the daughter of a third-generation furniture manufacturer. The family owned a stately Tudor home in Ridgetop, a house with Oriental carpets, Bavarian crystal, original oil paintings in golden frames, and a Pierce-Arrow in the driveway. A live-in housekeeper prepared and served the meals. A full-time butler mixed drinks from behind a mirrored bar.

When Merrilee was seven or eight years old, she skipped out to the back yard one day and ran smack into her guardian angel. She always maintained it was a real angel, one who floated in silence a moment above the sidewalk before disappearing.

My mother was long-limbed like her father, a dark-haired beauty like her mother. She was a naïve and shy girl but also intelligent and opinionated. She graduated from Washington University with a degree in English Literature and soon caught the eye of a handsome young engineer from New York, a fellow with a gregarious personality. He took her to a dance at the Chase Park Plaza Hotel. It was 1944, springtime, wartime. They fell for each other like a ton of bricks. In June the following year, they were married. The twenty-two-year-old bride wore Venetian lace. The groom wore his Navy dress whites. The reception was at Ridgetop. Then, during their brief honeymoon in Chicago, the groom's mother died unexpectedly. Two days after the wrenching funeral, he returned to duty at sea. When the war ended, Bob and Merrilee Underhill settled in St. Louis for life.

Mother was a woman of indomitable constitution, and she expected her children to be so endowed. She dealt with us deftly when we took sick but did not cosset or coddle. Instead, she encouraged us to get over our malady swiftly and stoically. She did not tolerate complainers, and she had little use for bored children. That first summer in Outer Mongolia, Mom's daily itinerary for her three oldest children began with plucking rocks from the gully-riven hardpack that was our front yard and moved on to pushing our youngest brother around the neighborhood in a stroller. When we returned, presuming we were finally free, Mom would hand us the car-wash bucket, a small mountain of silver to polish, or a book. Her frequent trips to the public library advanced our reading material from Nancy Drew to Pearl S. Buck and then on to Margaret Mitchell, Taylor Caldwell, and Ayn Rand.

She was a woman suited to graceful pastimes rather than competitions. In summer, she often took us to a complex of suburban swimming pools called Tree Court. While the other moms only dipped their toes in one of the warm-water pools, committed to preserving their bouffant hairdos, our mom buckled the chin strap of a bathing cap adorned with plastic flowers and executed a tidy dive into the ice-cold, spring-fed pool. There, in arctic solitude, she swam laps with the fluid movements of a seal.

She consistently hit hundred-and-twenty-yard drives, high, arcing shots that rarely veered off-center on the golf course. On the tennis courts, her long, tan arms executed reliable shots with a steady precision that was more lethal than the erratic killer strokes of her opponents.

Her fingers spanned ten piano keys with ease, lending smoothness to her renditions of "Claire de Lune" and "Tea for Two." She loved live theater and pops concerts, float trips down rivers with sand bars, peppermint ice cream with chocolate sauce, the color pink, *The Sound of Music*, bourbon Old Fashioneds, walks along the Fripp Island beach with her grandchildren, walks to the end of the Thornhill cul de sac with Dad.

She had a crush on Johnny Depp. She loved every pope, and both presidents named Bush. Over the years, she worked on political campaigns, organized bus tours of area churches, and read books to incarcerated youths. But her lasting calling was to advance the cause of natural family planning. Many weeknights, Mom returned to Thornhill well after dark, having driven miles to speak to a handful of nurses or to counsel a young couple about their family planning options. Among our most cherished treasures is a photograph taken at a Natural Family Planning conference in Guatemala. The headliner was Mother Teresa of Calcutta. As the flashbulb fired, Mother Teresa took our mother's hand and enfolded it in her own. The resulting photo shows two women who were called to different paths beaming at one another for a heartbeat.

Mom loved to entertain, and she did so often and with flair, with a small sprig of parsley decorating each square patty of butter and dinner plates warmed in the oven. Many a Sunday night, she invited a priest for supper, and out would come the good silver and her wedding dishes.

She attended Mother of Perpetual Help devotions on Tuesday nights, prayed at the Carmelite monastery on her knees, made pilgrimages to the Our Lady of the Snows Shrine in Illinois, and once to Fatima in Portugal. She kept a rosary in her handbag, another in the front hall cabinet, and yet another at her bedside.

She knew the Latin names of flowers, the streets of old St. Louis, the lives of the saints. She played a sharp game of bridge. She cheated brazenly and without remorse at Scrabble. She read the *Wall Street Journal* and *Value Line* daily and discussed her investments astutely. She loved to travel.

Mom wasn't perfect. She wasn't above swatting a bird dog, hard, if the dog snatched a pie off the kitchen counter. Her brownies were so formidable she had to chisel them out of the pan with a carving knife. And boy, could she pout.

After her children were grown, there were few things Mother enjoyed more than putting on a dress, spangling herself in jewelry, slipping into high heels, and driving off with Dad for an evening of dancing at the Casa Loma Ballroom.

They would sit at a cozy table in a pool of light from a tiny, shaded lamp, and watch dancers swirl and glide. With a bit of coaxing, Dad would escort Mom onto the dance floor. He would be a handsome young Navy lieutenant again, and she a shy and pampered girl.

On the last day of my mother's life, a pale winter sun melted into the horizon at 4:39 in the afternoon. Four hours later, behind clouds heavy with snow, a full moon coursed skies dotted with stars. Comets flared. Planets spun. It's possible—anything's possible—that flights of angels swept down on wings of glass to bear the soul of Merrilee Underhill to a place where time melts away and forever stays.

WHEN I FINISH speaking, I take my place in the pew beside Dennis and my daughters, utterly spent. Claire holds my hand in hers. After a few minutes, I stop listening to the familiar drone of a priest saying Mass. In my head, I hear Shirley singing again.

Slowly I unclench my fist.

I stay in St. Louis a few days to pack boxes and take pictures at Thornhill, for most of the rooms are still furnished much as they were years ago when the house rang with the sounds of six rambunctious children. As the hours pass, I am amazed at all the hospital-grade equipment and supplies required to keep her in the house she loved as long as possible: a wheelchair and wood ramp from the den door into the garage, a footed cane and a walker, oxygen condensers, masks, diapers, a shower chair, heating pads in every room, a hospital bed, a lift chair. Tubes of oinment. Surgical bandages. A long row of cinnamon-colored prescription bottles. A fat, three-ring binder filled with pages of caregiver notes and instructions.

Before starting to fill a Goodwill box with Mother's clothes, I hesitate. Three years ago, after Dad died, I took on the task of donating his clothes to a local charity. It felt intrusive, going through the pockets and discovering all the small items a person keeps in them. I remember sinking my hand into the pocket of his L.L. Bean field jacket and pulling out the remnants of an Oreo cookie, a treat he always brought along on quail hunting afternoons with one of the Patsies. His dog would not get the treat if she had run off to chase butterflies and go on point for bumble bees perched on purple coneflowers. And so that leftover cookie was evidence that my father's last autumn outing had been an exercise in frustration.

It's gotten late. A low afternoon sun is casting long shadows across the brick patio out back. I'll take care of packing Mother's clothes another day. I don't think I can bear discovering what a sweet, old lady has tucked into them, and left forever behind. I phone Tom for a ride back to his condo. By the time I see the headlights of his car, I have wept an ocean of tears.

Did any of my siblings ever think that once, just once, "the strong one" might not be?

Yes. That night, Paul sends an email with his thanks.

"I owe you dinner in St. Louis next time we're in," he writes.

Once again, I tell myself: *Surely the worst is over.*

I wish I could believe it.

On the day after the funeral, Tom gets a call from J.C. Penney's loss prevention department. Someone just charged $3,190 at Penney's using one of Mom's card numbers. Tom immediately freezes all of Mom's accounts, but it's too late to prevent our farewell checks to LaVerne and Shirley from bouncing.

What a mess.

The following day I'm back at Thornhill again to pack boxes when the kitchen phone rings. I pick up.

"Uh, Mrs. Underhill?"

"Who is this?

Click.

I'm sure it was the woman who stole Mom's credit card information. My heart pounds with fear. She knows the address. She is calling to see if the house is empty. If I hadn't picked up, we might have had another break-in.

This family is living under a cloud! First, a homeless man trashes every room in our family home. Then, an identity thief cashes in on our mother's line of credit. And now, some lowlife is checking to see if the place is empty so they can steal what's left of value here.

I phone Dennis in Milwaukee. He asks what he's supposed to do from four hundred miles away. *I don't know. Calm me down. Tell me it'll be okay.*

He doesn't. But he does summon Meg, and within half an hour, her car is pulling up the drive at Thornhill. In time, we will learn that the woman who used Mother's credit card number at Penney's is part of a multi-state identity theft ring. After being taken into federal custody, she told authorities she was alerted to the death through the obituary we placed in the *St. Louis Post-Dispatch*.

The Underhills are not a Norman Rockwell family. This Christmas season, snarky emails are flying, and the blades are out.

Matt wishes us a Merry Christmas. He says we are losing control just like we did after Dad died. It's our temperaments, he says. We're not easy. He tells us that losing Mom so close to the holidays, and not being with her at the end, has hit him particularly hard.

Tom tells me to give myself a well-deserved pat on the back for all that I did to honor our mother and father. He advises me to not seek or expect any thanks from two of our siblings and not take their criticism seriously.

I apologize to everyone in the family for everything I ever did, ever said, ever thought in my entire life. Afterward, I don't feel one iota better.

On the afternoon of New Year's Eve, Tom drives to Thornhill to check on the empty house. When our driveway is in sight, he sees a car parked in front of our garage.

"Here we go again," he tells himself, tensing.

Tom pulls up the drive and parks. Taking care to stand by the open door of his car, he scans the familiar rows of windows along the front of the house, envisioning the interior of each room. He glances at the front door, flanked by pots of geraniums withered to stalks. Hears the rope halyard, stiff from the cold, clanking against the metal flagpole with each gust of wind. Finally, he walks around the side of the house, where he can see the back patio and yard. In the gloaming, he spots a man standing the edge of the hill that drops steeply to the valley where years ago we blazed trails through stands of Queen Anne's Lace.

For a beat or two, the man doesn't move. Then, he turns toward the creek where the Underhill kids splashed in muddy rills and plucked arrowheads from rocky shoals on the first day of our first summer in Outer Mongolia.

Tom watches the man blow on his hands and stuff them in the pockets of his corduroy overcoat.

Still, he doesn't turn around.

Tom's worried now. He has no idea who the man is or what might be in a pocket of that corduroy coat. A handgun? A knife? When the man lowers his head as if debating with himself, Tom swallows a wave of anxiety and takes a step closer. The grass is crisp with frost. Surely the man will either pivot and confront him or run down the hill toward Manchester Road.

The guy doesn't move.

It's strange, Tom tells himself. It's as if the guy hasn't heard a thing.

Tom closes the distance between them by half and then stops. Nothing. Finally, my brother gives a sharp whistle, and the guy spins around.

Relief washes over Tom. He flings his arms wide and calls out, "Charlie!"

Our cousin, Charlie Meier, breaks into a broad grin.

Charlie has been deaf since birth. His speech is difficult for us to understand. Charlie did not use American Sign Language, but that hardly mattered because none of us bothered to learn it. I do not think any of us ever had a substantive conversation with him, yet he was kind and gentle, good-natured about our failure to understand his words, and always a part of the rambunctious holiday mix of kids with whom we shared our holidays. If he was disappointed that we never took the time or made the effort to get to know him well, he did not show it.

Charlie and Tom whack each other on the shoulders the way men do. Finally, he taps Tom's arm and indicates he'd like to go inside the house.

Charlie walks slowly through the first floor of the house. From time to time, he stops to look at something that had been special for him—the family photographs on the wall in Dad's den, the glass candlesticks on the dining room table, the gun cabinet he made as a thank-you gift after Dad included him on bird-hunting outings.

Out on the driveway, the cousins stand by their cars, shuffling their feet in the bitter cold, not knowing exactly how to end things. Finally, they shake hands. Tom is fishing for his car keys when he feels another tap on the shoulder.

With darkness falling fast, with clouds skimming overhead and the biting scent of snow in the air, Charlie looks off, seeming to gather himself. Then he turns back to Tom. Enunciating as clearly as bells pealing in a church tower, Charlie says,

"So many memories."

Chapter 35
Lists and Directives
2007

An assortment of colored dots

WE HAVE LAID our mother to rest beside our father. We have left their crises and issues behind. Now, finally, we can move on in unity and harmony.

But we don't. We lawyer up.

When an old disagreement about who will direct the disbursal of our parents' personal effects flares again, Paul says he's willing to discuss the matter with Yves, the family's new lawyer.

"What kind of name is that?" Tom asks me.

"No clue. Maybe the guy's French."

I mail a thick packet to maybe-French Yves. It contains copies of all the lists and directives my parents drew up over the years, in particular the ones that support my appointment to the role Paul is contesting. Yves replies that he has received the packet. Period.

Meanwhile, we propose various procedures for selecting the things from the house that we want. Take turns in age-order. Take turns in reverse age order. Draw straws for each round. Assign items to their logical recipient.

Paul says Yves says the lists I sent are not worth the paper Mother and Dad wrote them on.

Paul goes on to say it's clear to him our mother was unduly influenced. And he's still simmering about Mom's gifts of jewelry over the years to Pam and me.

I phone Yves. In the spirit of international diplomacy, I open with, "Bonjour, monsieur."

Yves replies, "Who's calling?"

So much for my attempt at Gallic rapport. I ask Yves for an update on my parents' lists and directives. He tells me he cannot counsel me or represent me because he represents Mother's estate, and thus, he is obliged to deal only with its co-executors, Paul and Tom.

With that, Pam and I are stripped of the last responsibility our parents wanted us to hold.

Paul prepares a spreadsheet detailing mother's assets and sends it to each of us with an initial distribution of funds. He adds that there isn't much left of Mom's extensive jewelry collection in the estate.

That's baloney. There's plenty. Cripes, you would think Pam and I reduced our mother from Liz Taylor to The Little Match Girl!

We agree to meet in March at Thornhill. The house has been uninhabited for months. It's kind of creepy, but Paul and I decide to stay there anyway. Early on the day of the meeting, he sets up chairs in the family room and I run a vacuum.

In years past, we sat with our cousins on the floor here, cheating with impunity at Monopoly after holiday meals. My sister and I dragged blankets and pillows from our bedrooms for slumber parties in this room. Paul and Tom wrestled like bear cubs on the long sofa here, inevitably tumbling off to soft landings on the rug I'm vacuuming. Ken's preferred position for television-watching here would be to flop onto his stomach on the floor and rest his chin in his cupped hands. It was the cue for the current Patsy to finish licking the last scrap from her dog bowl, settle down perpendicular to Ken, and lay her head in the small of his back. After all the Patsies came and went, Dad's willful German shorthair, a hellion he named Heidi, would fart herself to sleep at our father's feet here while Dad channel-surfed for C-Span, or a John Wayne movie. In later years, Pam's children and mine and then Paul's, Ken's, and Matt's would tiptoe downstairs on Christmas mornings and root through gifts piled under a tree dropping the first of its needles on the dusty rose rug I am vacuuming for the last time.

Threads of late winter sunlight splash across the room, from the chair where Mother read the morning paper until lunchtime to the chair where Dad sawed logs during the *The Late, Late Show*.

Pam bails again. Tom arrives looking pasty and announces he's got diarrhea. Matt flew in hard upon a root canal. Ken's late.

Paul welcomes everyone. He makes a beautiful opening statement without a trace of smug bravado and then opens his laptop. I see a spreadsheet on the screen. My hand clenches.

What happens next takes my breath away:

Civility. Impartiality. Generosity. Kinship. Nostalgia.

"We'll go in birth order," Paul begins, "and at some point, we'll put Pam's name on things we think she'd want. Cath, you're up first."

There it is—the sudden, astonishing end to the titanic power struggle of alpha siblings. After years of distrust and positioning, Paul had won and took no advantage. I had lost and accepted it. In that moment, the resentments of the past dissipated. The distrust, gone, if not entirely forgotten.

I get right to it; this chummy new Underhill zeitgeist could revert to true any minute.

I select a picture with an appraised value of about $200. It is a print of a French chateau that hung over the mantel in the Chafford Woods house and, later, in the living room at Thornhill. Since my earliest years, I have loved its golden pastels and dreamy scenery.

"Oh," Paul says under his breath, "I sort of wanted that." He bows his head and types my name in the appropriate line on the spreadsheet.

"Who's next?" he says, looking up again, his voice bright. "Me, I guess."

That morning, without a hint of disagreement, we parcel out what our parents took in over their lifetimes.

During a break for lunch, I think about the process Paul selected, how it is fair but not impartial. In each round, I realize, I get to select something before anyone else does, before Paul does.

Pam writes to thank us. She says she plans to buy a much bigger house in a year or so, and she will display things from Thornhill there. She says she will enjoy having us visit her in the years to come. In her dreamlike conjuring of the future and in light of her emotional instability, I find my sister's note particularly sad.

A month after the meeting, we resume our natural state of epistolary disagreement and quibble about every aspect of the sale of the Thornhill house. The asking price, the realtor's commission, whether to negotiate on a counteroffer, all are reasonably in play. But things get ugly when we learn that the primary bidders intend to tear the house down and build on the property. They are medical doctors from India, a husband and wife.

Paul says "some of us" are just out for quick money. He says he doesn't want to sound maudlin, but he would like to stand over our parents' graves and know that we tried our best to leave their home in good hands. There are undercurrents here, and they are not pretty.

Ken takes his older brother to task. He asks if we are meant to restrict prospective buyers to a Caucasian, married with children, Roman Catholic, politically conservative, and a dog lover.

I wade in.

"Based on Mom and Dad's current whereabouts, I assume they would not consider predicating a sale on a buyer's ethnicity, skin color, religion, or voting record."

Paul is undaunted. He says his children will be despondent when they return to St. Louis, drive out to Thornhill, and see a hole in the ground. He says they'll have to hold up an old picture of the house to remember what it looked like.

He says at this time of year he works twelve-hour days and concedes that he is physically and emotionally exhausted. He advises us to approve "the damn deal."

Tom tells me he doesn't care if the buyer lives at Thornhill or tears it down. He says he find the place depressing compared with his wonderful early years there.

I wish the new owners would tear the place down and rebuild. That way, we would be the only family to have ever lived there.

In early May, Matt asks if I will participate in an intervention for Ken. Dennis is against it, but I can't bring myself to say no. I am beginning to realize this is a thing with me, saving people whom I believe need me to save them. Matt and I know something must be done to help Ken, but for now an intervention is on hold.

A St. Louis friend from my days at the *Globe-Democrat* recommends an estate sale firm to sell the dregs we left at the house. The first thing to go is the chair lift. The last thing is a small plastic bin. Our net proceeds are $6,000.

On the evening of the estate sale, I sit curled in a chair in my Hidden Reserve house, the house Dennis and I built, and I think about Thornhill, the house my parents built, the house they lived in for more than forty years. They loved that house. They would not leave it, ever, would not bow to the limitations of age and infirmity, did not fear the likelihood of an accident there, and refused to cede to the will of a daughter who thought it best to remove them from their home.

I guess that's not unusual, but still, it's remarkable.

The real estate agent lives in Thornhill Estates. After we close on the house sale, I write to her.

Dear Patty,

How I wish you could have been here in the early years. We were the third family to build in Thornhill. My dad paid $32,000 for the house and the lot. While it was being built, he wouldn't let my mother come out to see the progress. He was worried she would want a bunch of luxury upgrades. Poor dear.

Directly behind our lot was an old white frame farmhouse at the end of a dirt lane. The same family had owned it for generations. Their water came from an outdoor cistern. Can you imagine the squabbles over hot water for shampoos? There were always cats and kittens roaming the place, and I remember the mother canned fruit and baked wonderful pies. Eventually, they sold the land to a developer who wanted to expand Thornhill Estates. The family arranged to have their farmhouse lifted off its original stone foundation and moved down the road. What a process! Back then, a walk down that road led to Charlie's Country Store and bins of candy.

Our front yard that first summer was a sea of mud. Each morning, Mom made her older kids pick rocks out of the soil to prepare it for the first application of seeds. Eventually, the grass took hold. It was the end of the Cold War years, and Dad always claimed he would dig a space for a bomb shelter in our back yard where it drops off precipitously. Did he think the Underhills would be the sole survivors of a nuclear holocaust?

During our first summers at Thornhill, my sister and I pushed our younger brothers in strollers up to Topping Road to get the mail each day. The drone of dump trucks and the tap-tap of hand-held hammers were the ambient sound of our world, a world we called Outer Mongolia.

Later, horses nickered in the Thornhill stables across from the pool. In Spring, as soon as the pool was filled with water, we dove in. We never tired of hopping along the raised stepstones between the kiddie pool and the main basin.

My brothers and sister and I volleyed for hours on the Thornhill tennis courts. And the pool parties back then often got out of hand. After dark, while the parents danced and drank, clusters of kids spied on them from behind nearby bushes, laughing into our cupped hands when someone's dad or mom fell into the pool.

We will never forget our years at Thornhill. It was a house built for us, and as long as it stands, it was home to only us.

Warm regards,

Catherine [15]

Chapter 36
Love and Lightning
August 2009

At dawn, the wind picks up

ON A HILLTOP stippled with century-old hardwoods and late summer wildflowers, a handful of guests chat with one another, taking care to keep well back from a precipice where the land falls sharply away. Below, waves bubble up to a rocky shoreline and recede again. The day is waning, the rhythm of the water slowing. In hours, the great lake will smooth to glass.

A young man in a dark suit and gleaming shoes clasps his hands behind him. He appears calm. He is not. Now and then, he bobs lightly on the balls of his feet, the giveaway. At last, he hears the crunch of footfalls on a wood-chip trail. He looks up. Everyone looks up.

She has arrived, my Claire.

His Claire.

They are as unlike as can be, this wedding couple.

Mary Claire Fitzpatrick, her hair and complexion fair, her soft features dominated by enormous dove-gray eyes that belie a powerful disposition. Claire flashes with passion and bleeds with compassion.

She is sometimes as giddy as a child and often wicked-funny. Gregarious, capricious, and generous. A planner inclined to spontaneity. Her father and I suspect the admixture is the result of her Irish, Scottish, English, and German ancestry.

Daniel Eugene Gould, tall and handsome, broad through the shoulders, easy to tan. His hair and eyes are chestnut brown. His posture would satisfy a Marine drillmaster. In disposition, Dan is steady as a metronome. Within his bones, he carries the aspirations of his Jewish ancestors who, generations ago, risked all they had to escape the oppression of Eastern Europe and bought passage on ships bound for America. America! with its tantalizing promise of hope. His mother is a teacher. His father owned a pharmacy and a toy store. Lucky boy, Dan.

Among the few guests invited to witness the vow ceremony, I dare say no one doubts this fusion of opposites will hold fast.

And yet, the day got off to a bumpy start. Shortly after dawn, a storm boiled over Door County, the long point of land that for generations has been Wisconsin's most-loved vacation destination. In summer, picturesque villages, shops, and supper clubs bubble with tourists who come for a week at a quaint resort, an open-air fish boil, an afternoon in an orchard or a winery, and a Swedish pancake at Al Johnson's, where goats nibble grass on the rooftop.

At dawn, the wind picks up. Thunder and lightning sweep across the peninsula. Rain needles the windowpanes of the historic Whistling Swan Inn in Fish Creek, wedding central.

In the bridal suite, Claire storms into the bathroom and slams the door. Meg belays bulletins to interested parties in the hallway. She hears faucets turning, water running into the clawfoot tub, and her sister describing the weather in technicolor terms.

After an hour, Dennis goes in search of the groom.

For most of the morning, Dan has been sitting on the covered front porch of the Whistling Swan, awaiting delivery of the custom-tailored suit he ordered for this day. He has tracked on the Internet the journey of his wedding suit from Hong Kong to a port of entry in America. On the day before the wedding, customs released the suit, and a courier service flew it to Milwaukee. From Fish Creek, Dan made panicked arrangements for a courier to drive the suit to the Whistling Swan Inn, a journey of three hours. Ever since breakfast, Dan has kept a glum vigil on the stoop, watching rain fall on tourists dashing from shop to shop. Each time he sees a vehicle that might be a delivery truck, he jumps up. Each time it continues on without stopping, he slumps. Fortunately, he packed a spare suit for just-in-case. That's Dan.

Dennis accompanies his future son-in-law up the winding wood staircase. At the door to the bridal suite, they part ways. From the hallway, I hold my breath as Dan risks a gingerly knock on the bathroom door. "Honey, you coming out?"

The response nearly blows the door off its hinges. Claire intends to stay in the bathroom until the skies clear.

In the early afternoon, Dan's wedding suit finally arrives, and the storm departs. Hallelujah!

Claire emerges, wrapped in a hotel towel, her skin pinked and wrinkled. She steps into the elegant, satin wedding gown she snagged on J.Crew's clearance page. At my suggestion, we had a seamstress remove strands of French Alençon lace from my wedding gown and hand-stitch them across the front of Claire's bias-cut dress. The finishing touch is a spectacular diamond pendant in the shape of a comet. It hangs from a slender silver chain around her neck and catches the afternoon light. I inherited the treasure from my mother. She inherited it from her mother. Now, it is Claire's.

Claire and Dan exchange vows in Peninsula State Park, standing under an eggshell-blue sky and a canopy of sugar maple, basswood, and beech trees. After the brief ceremony, Dan's father withdraws from his suit pocket a small glass light bulb wrapped in a white cloth and hands it to Dan, who smashes it underfoot, symbolizing the finality of the marriage covenant and I recite the traditional Irish blessing. Before I get to the part about God holding them in the palm of His hand, my voice quavers with emotion.

After the last kiss and handshake, the last photograph and wish for a long and happy life, the Fitzpatrick-Gould wedding party returns to the Whistling Swan for champagne and supper. One mile northeast of the inn, dusk falls soft across a clearing stippled with wildflowers where, this very day, a young woman with grey eyes and soft features and a young man with broad shoulders vowed to love one another all the days of their lives.

Below the bluff, low waves march in cadence to a ribbon of stones worn to velvet, and a westering sun gilds the tranquil bay with flecks of amber.

During the drive back to Milwaukee, I burst out crying with the realization that if Claire is in a car accident, we are no longer her closest relatives.

"You're right," Dennis says, handing me a Kleenex. "If our daughter wrecks another car, Dan will get the call, not us."

After a pause, we both smile.

Chapter 37
My sister!
Autumn 2009

I see her in silhouette

MY SISTER CALLS. I haven't spoken to her in months. Haven't wanted to.

"Cath-eee, I don't think I'm going to make it!"

Her voice is high and thin, each word elongated and shrill as a dentist's drill. The sound turns my blood to ice.

Dennis and I are expecting ten guests for dinner. They're due to arrive in an hour.

I speak in a soft, comforting tone and choose my words carefully.

"Don't worry, Pam. I'm coming. I'll come to you. I will fly to Ithaca tomorrow."

I tell her to leave her front door unlocked. I warn her that if I travel halfway across the country and stand on her doorstep, locked out, I will not be happy. She agrees. I ask for the phone number of her doctor and she gives it to me. When she finally seems calmer, I tell her I love her, and we hang up.

Through the night, she calls repeatedly. The couples at our table are our friends for a reason: they are sympathetic and understanding. After they leave, I send word to my brothers.

> Catherine – Hello, all. Pam has spiraled into a critical medical and psychological state that poses an imminent danger to her. I have spoken with her many times. I have contacted the oldest of Pam's children. This afternoon, I talked to Pam's psychologist (with her permission), and with her friend in Ithaca. I am flying to Ithaca tomorrow morning. Pam's son will get there the following day.

Paul answers with a nice note. Matt writes too; he muses about how sad it is when a family looks back after a tragedy and recalls the signals the person in trouble sent, reaching for a lifeline, but the family took no action. He thanks me for taking steps to get help for Pam.

I tell Matt I expect him to have a talk with God. What I don't say is that I am guilty of keeping distance between my sister and me for more than a year.

Guilty as sin.

In distancing myself from Pam, I broke the solemn pledge I gave my parents long ago to shore her up when she needed it, to have her back in challenging times.

The failures here are not my sister's. I underestimated the psychological disease that strained her marriage, affected her children, restricted her ability to travel, prevented her from keeping promises she desperately wanted to keep, and tore her to pieces. I saw only my mother's disappointments and my inconveniences, not the terrible inner struggles Pam tried to overcome, or at least to hide. I expected of her what she was unable to give. All the while, she was silently crying out for help.

I failed my parents. I failed my sister and everyone who loved her. So did our parents, who decades ago should have sought a clinical diagnosis for their fragile child's mercurial temperament. Her teachers, who should have alerted the family to her social impairment. Her husband, whose frustrations led to quarrels. And especially the doctors and counselors, who did but little and followed up even less.

It makes me sick at heart.

On Monday, Oct. 5, I get to Ithaca in the early afternoon. At the front door of my sister's home, I raise a hand knotted in a tight ball. But instead of knocking, I give the door a nudge, and it opens.

"Pam?"

Nothing.

Then, louder, "Pam?"

I look in the living room, the dinette, the kitchen, and the guest bath. I look in the three upstairs bedrooms, behind the shower curtain, in closets. I start to tremble. Basement. Garage.

Years ago, Pam and her husband had a contractor finish the lower level of the house as a rec room, with carpeting, lamps, a television, and a desk. I find her there, lying on her side, knees to chin, on a plaid sofa. She raises her head and begins to rock and keen.

"My sister! My sister! My sister's come!"

I shrug out of my coat and kneel beside the couch.

She is wearing a thin nightgown, nothing else. Her hair is unwashed and messy. Her lips are cracked and bleeding. She is thinner than I've ever seen her. The skin of her arms and legs is marbled. I realize that aside from unlocking the front door, she has not moved, eaten, or taken any liquids since our phone call, eighteen hours ago.

I rub her shoulders, pull strands of hair from her face, and tuck a blanket over her. That done, I hurry upstairs to the kitchen and return with a cup of orange juice and a straw. She manages a small sip. I encourage her to take another, but she gags on it and slumps back down.

Her laptop computer is open on the desk. On the screen is a Word document. I look closer; she has been revising her will.

Pam sighs and closes her eyes. When she is dozing, I sit at the desk, open her email account, and write to my brothers again: "I am with Pam. Our sister is dying. You must come."

I tell them our nephew, Patrick, Pam's older son, is flying to Ithaca tomorrow. I tell them Patrick and I have a plan: We will drive Pam to Patrick's home in Kentucky and get her into in-patient treatment there. Pam's daughter, Elise, and younger son, David, have offered encouragement.

Pam wakes. Although she is groggy, I question her about how she came to be in such dire condition. In a weak, halting voice, she mumbles an appalling answer. When she falls asleep again, I send an update to my brothers.

> Catherine – Pam is in terrible shape. She has told me that in the past few days she has tried to end her life by taking an overdose of prescription medicine with bourbon, and then by starvation. Also, I see slash marks on her wrist. She is critical.

Behind me, Pam stirs. Quickly, I cross the room to her. I encourage her to rouse herself a bit, take another sip of juice. When I suggest we go to the hospital, she flies into a frenzy of desperation, and I panic. I cannot risk losing her trust, so I resolve to let her stay at home, at least for a while.

I brought with me a dozen snapshots of our early childhood years in Chafford Woods. My coat and handbag are on the floor, where I tossed them when I arrived. I rummage my purse for the photos, and we pass a nostalgic half-hour looking at ourselves in simpler, happier times. I make toast and tea and bring it down. She takes a bite from the edge. She seems calmer.

Dusk brings a sudden, dramatic change. Without warning, Pam flings off the blanket. In a burst of excitement, she demands I go upstairs with her. When she stands up, I see how thin she's become. I tell her to stay on the couch a little longer, tell her I'll fix her an egg or cereal. Her eyes flash with anger, and I back off.

She goes directly upstairs to her bedroom and flings open the drawers of a large bureau. Carefully, lovingly, she withdraws an astonishing collection of designer clothes. A cocktail dress encrusted with beads and sequins. A gorgeous Gorsuch ski jacket, the label favored by celebrities and royals. She opens her closet, pulls out expensive clothes by the handful, and tosses them on the bed for me to admire. I wrote about fashion trends for years; I know the designers. My sister has bought a wardrobe sufficient for a woman at the highest levels of society, and yet she is barely able to leave her house.

"Do you have places to wear these things?" I ask, trying to keep my voice neutral.

"Oh, I get out all the time. I go to the store for food. I go to my dance aerobics classes, sometimes twice a day. I take walks."

"Pam, how did you get all these things? Did you go to New York?"

She smiles. "Oh, I just call my personal shopper at Bergdorf's."

Of course. And the person on the other end of the line is extremely happy to help.

With obvious pride, she tells me she is down to a Size 8. She's not. A Size 4 would hang on her.

As quickly as she left the malaise of the basement behind for the euphoria of a wardrobe reveal upstairs, she abruptly switches focus again.

"We're French, you know," she says, staring at me intently.

"We are?"

"Dad always said we're English, but we're not. We're French."

"How's that?"

My sister took Spanish in high school, and long afterward she dreamed about one day visiting Spain. In more recent years, though, Pam has immersed herself in French language lessons. Before her illness became acute, she was taking advanced courses at the university level. She had become so fluent she could read French language books and watch French films without subtitles.

"Our ancestry is completely French through Dad's mother," she insists, standing close, speaking with odd urgency. "I researched it all, and it's true. Her maiden name was Alice Marie Larrivee. Her parents came from France to Eastern Canada. Back then, if the immigration agents couldn't pronounce or spell a name, they just gave the person the surname L'Arrivee. It means, 'the arriver.'"

"Okay, that makes sense." At this point, I will agree with anything.

Pam is on the move again. In one of the spare bedrooms, she drops to her knees and begins opening boxes of paperwork. All the while, she continues to spin threads of conjecture about our French ancestry, speaking faster and faster, imploring me to tell our brothers, to write it all down, to make sure all the Underhills know that we are French.

"I will," I assure her. "I'll tell them."

I have no memory of that night's dinner. Cereal. Or frozen pizza. By the time I unpack my things in a bedroom down the hall, I'm exhausted. I hear Pam in the bathroom, brushing her teeth, getting ready for bed. Quietly, I make my way to the basement and dash off another email to Dennis and my brothers. I tell them I will be alone in the house with Pam. I confide to them that I expect a tough night.

It is.

Around midnight, Pam barges into the bedroom and hovers over me until I sense her presence and wake up with a jolt. Moonlight streams through the window. I see her in silhouette, shaking with fury.

"How could you tell me you didn't want to hear from me anymore," she shouts. "Why did you do that, Cathy? WHY?"

She bends over me, breathing hard, eager for a response that will serve to ramp up her anger. I have no idea what to say, so I say nothing. My terrified silence further enrages her. She backs off, pacing the room, shouting wild accusations. Eventually, she tires. I tell her I'm exhausted. I remind her I've come all the way from Wisconsin today to see her, and now I need sleep. Somehow, it de-escalates the ugly scene. Pam recedes to her room. I close the door to mine. There's no lock. I fish in my purse and find my phone and call my husband. My heart is pounding. The image of an airplane spearing into a skyscraper flashes before my eyes.

"I'm scared," I whisper into the phone. "It's like being alone in a house with a wild animal."

"Leave!" Dennis shouts. "Call a cab. Go to a hotel. Then come home!"

I stay.

Tuesday, October 6

Pam is up early. She's brewed coffee, poured juice, made toast. To pass the time before Patrick, her son, arrives, I suggest we wash the few dishes together like we did when we were girls at Thornhill, and then take a walk.

"You wash, I'll dry," I say.

"No, you wash, and I'll dry," she answers, and we laugh. It was our familiar call and response.

The autumn morning is clear and crisp. We amble along—she's still frail and unsteady, but the fresh air and exercise revive her. She guides me along her regular route and points out the houses of the few neighbors she knows by name. I start to think the morning will go smoothly when, unexpectedly, she launches into an angry monolog about politics. I listen in silence until she refers to the president and first lady in crass, racist terms. I have never heard my sister use base language. I have never known her to think in such derogatory terms. It's as if a switch has flipped, turning Pam into someone different. She walks on and I follow. I tell her I don't want to listen to that kind of talk. She merely laughs off her crude tirade, turns her face to the sun, and asks me if this isn't the most glorious October day ever.

I steer her toward home. Patrick will be there by now.

My nephew is tall and fit, a kind-hearted man with a wife and a demanding career in Kentucky. When we walk into the house, he is standing at the dinette table, finishing a cup of coffee.

Pam flies into a rage. She accuses Patrick and me of deceiving her, which we did. Of plotting against her. True. Of over-dramatizing her condition. We have not.

Terrified that we will force her into "an insane asylum," she lashes at Patrick in visceral language. He cowers under the barrage but knows to keep quiet, wait it out. Soon, his sick and starved mother has backed him into a corner of the room.

Finally, Pam is spent. Patrick and I work in tandem to convince her to get help, at least to see her psychologist. Worn from her tirade, she agrees. Surely, I say to myself, the man will realize my sister is dangerously ill. Surely, he will convince her to enter in-patient treatment.

Pam washes and styles her hair. She applies makeup and puts on a pretty wool skirt, sweater, hose, and heels. The transformation is astonishing, and purposefully deceptive.

Patrick and I ask her if we can attend the session with her, and she agrees.

That afternoon, the three of us cram into the man's small office. For the next half-hour, my sister whispers and shouts, weeps and laughs nervously, answers in single syllables or not at all, fidgets, and wrings her hands. Twice she leaps up and marches out into the hall, threatening to leave. Twice Patrick and I reel her back in. The psychologist, a man of about forty-five with thinning hair and delicate hands, gives no indication he is aware that my sister's condition is grave.

"Now, Pam," he says more than once, "when you go home, what's your plan?"

I want to scream. I want to vault over his desk and grab him by the shoulders and smack him.

What's her PLAN? Mister, Pam has no plan. Pam is going crazy right here in your office. What's YOUR plan, you incompetent wimp!

When Pam storms out for a third time, Patrick and I walk out, too. At the door, I turn and cut the man a look he could not mistake. He quickly looks down and fiddles with his pen.

That night, Patrick carries his small suitcase to the basement rec room. Pam and I turn in upstairs. A short while later, I hear my nephew opening and closing cabinets and drawers in the kitchen. Curious, I go down.

He is worried. He suspects his mother has hidden a butcher knife somewhere in the house.

With that, the room spins. I am quartered in a bedroom a few steps from a severely unstable woman experiencing wild mood swings she cannot control. She is resentful toward me. She has a butcher knife. And we can't find it.

"I have to go," I tell him. "Right now."

He understands. In the pitch of night, he drives me to a nearby hotel. On the way, we agree to try again tomorrow to get Pam to Kentucky.

Wednesday, October 7

Patrick picks me up first thing in the morning. At the house, I see Pam has dressed for a fifties-era cookbook photo, in a skirt and sweater, low heels, and a gingham cobbler apron. She pours coffee and sets out a platter of buttermilk biscuit warm from the oven.

"See?" she says, triumphant. "I'm fine."

She is not. By then, both Patrick and I have seen evidence that Pam has been drinking alcohol and swallowing prescription drugs at a self-destructive rate. We have also learned from a concerned neighbor and directly from Pam that during the past few weeks she has been treated more than once in the emergency room of an Ithaca hospital. We don't know the specifics. We only know that each time she refused to be admitted for psychological evaluation, and she was not admitted against her will. I guess irrational agitation, excessive drinking, abuse of prescription drugs, self-starvation, and eight to ten slash marks on her wrist do not qualify as being an imminent threat to the life of herself or others.

After breakfast, Patrick and I cautiously mention our plan. Oh no, Pam says, her voice rising. Absolutely not.

We reason with her. We argue and even joke with her. Pam keeps her composure and maintains her resolve. She promises to make another appointment with the psychologist, to follow his directions, and to take her medicine as prescribed. She tells us she will continue to exercise and pay close attention to a nutritious diet. She will get well, she says, and do so on her own terms.

We have lost the battle, for now.

I throw my clothes into the suitcase and wait by the window for the taxi to pull into the driveway. And with that, I am swiftly transported to the morning six years ago when I fled Thornhill, fearing I had been turned out. As in a dream, the scene abruptly changes. I am at the wheel of a car speeding toward the median strip of a Milwaukee highway. Another scene change. I am at the foot of a tall building, staring upward with arms outstretched. Empty jackets, dresses, shirts, and shoes flutter down, cast against a sky the color of bluebells.

Thursday, October 8

I email my brothers. I tell them Patrick returned to Kentucky and I am in Milwaukee and Pam is alone again. I tell them she is under the care of a psychologist, not a psychiatrist, and that the man is worthless. I add that although our sister was stable when I left, I have no confidence it will last.

> Catherine – Brothers, please step in. Assemble a professional intervention. Go there. Fly there. Be there. Your turn. Our Pam is just in pitiful shape, and I am wrung out.

Friday, October 9

Pam's daughter, Elise, contacts me. She's had a call from her mother. Pam is in turmoil. Elise says she's afraid her mother is "not going to make it."

"Are those your words or hers?"

"Hers."

I tell Elise that her Underhill aunt and uncles are planning an intervention. I assure her it will happen soon. I tell her to be ready.

Matt tells us he has made contacts. He recommends we get Pam to a private rehabilitation hospital on the East Coast that specializes in behavioral health care treatment. I look it up. The place is gorgeous, a rambling, white frame building set high on wooded grounds, with chimneys, gables, and lush gardens lined with low stone walls. It's the kind of place where money buys privacy, discretion, and dignity.

Matt hires an Arizona interventionist. My brothers and I agree to pay the man's fee and travel expenses.

I reach Pam by phone. She sounds terrible. She tells me she's finished a bottle of bourbon she bought two days ago, and she's eaten almost nothing.

"I have to hang up," she says abruptly. "I have to go throw up."

There are times when I ask myself why Pam's adult children are not leading the effort to get help for their mother, but I know the answer. Pam's illness wounded and depressed our mother. It inconvenienced and infuriated her siblings. But her children felt the pain of it longer and more acutely than did we, and at vulnerable ages. They grew up in the tumult that led to their parents' divorce. They lived with the heartache of a mother riddled with phobias, mood swings, and unreliability. They are as loving and attentive as they can be, but the raw ugliness of the illness has ground them down. I would guess they are desperate for us to succeed and terrified we will fail. We have their support and their prayers. It's enough.

What I am sorry about is Paul's harsh attitude. In an email, he asks us when Elise will arrive in Ithaca for the intervention. He demands Patrick get his ass to Ithaca, too. Paul's words. He says he doesn't care if being at the intervention will be difficult for them. He says they are partly responsible for the years their mother's condition was insufficiently treated, and for lax coordination between her immediate family and her doctors. He says Pam should never have been allowed to become so ill that she is at the brink of suicide.

Paul goes on to say that long ago his sister was incapable of directing her own medical care. He questions why that wasn't apparent to those closest to her. He says he doesn't give a rip about patient-friendly New York state laws; if necessary, he says, we should subdue Pam with restraints and forcibly transport her to the East Coast rehab center.

He's not done.

He says his business accounts are at a critical time of year and he cannot phone Pam and get into a harangue with her because afterward he would be too keyed up to do justice to his employees and clients, who need him. He says his world in Portland cannot come to a screaming halt because of his sister. He says if she killed herself this very day, he would not be able to be break free and get to the funeral.

He ends by saying that while the timing for him is inconvenient, postponing the intervention would make it too late to matter.

I don't believe a word my brother wrote. Paul loves her and he is scared. This is how he shows it.

This evening, I phone Elise. She and I make a list of things to do while she is in Ithaca for the intervention. I tell her what to pack for her mother. Together, we try to think of everything Pam will need or want during her treatment period. I wish Elise luck. I ask God to bless us all.

Elise asks about the cost. I tell her we will work out the financial arrangements later. I don't tell her that the beautiful treatment center with a view of the ocean requires $10,000 immediately upon admission and another $1,500 a day or $55,000 for a four-week course of treatment.

Saturday, October 10

Three days after I leave my sister's house, Ken and Matt arrive in Ithaca and check into a hotel. Elise and Patrick are there already.

That night in the hotel, Matt writes to remind all of us that we are blessed to be a family committed to each other and willing to make sacrifices for a loved one. He points out that Pam's children have endured tremendous stress and anguish over the years, but he is hopeful we are on the right path now. He asks for our prayers.

At home in Hidden Reserve, I write a letter to Pam and email it to Matt and Ken. I ask them to read it to Pam at the intervention.

Une letter a ma cher soeur,

I am not among the gathering of your loved ones today, but I am with you in spirit, in my thoughts, in my heart.

Through the years and especially in recent days, your deteriorating health has been an overriding concern to me. When I arrived at your house, your condition was shocking. We embraced, affection that was surely overdue. You felt you needed to tell me about Dad's French ancestors. In your mind, your research would be lost forever if you didn't pass it along to me right then, right there, and I realized that either your mind could not hold a single thought for more than a couple of minutes, or that you knew you did not have long to live. A terrible sickness had taken hold of you. At one point that night, you asked me to assist you in ending your life, and when I refused, you asked me to leave so that you could end your life.

I would not do that, either. I have too much love and respect for you. I have too many happy memories of our shared girlhood. And we have too many memories yet to make.

Cares mount up over the years. They come hand-in-hand with falling in love, marrying, having babies, pursuing a demanding but satisfying career. You have accomplished remarkable things. Along the way, you filled your heart with loved ones and filled your life with responsibilities. You handled yourself with grace and style, with vulnerability tempered by remarkable fortitude.

I am sick at heart for the love of you, Pam. My stay at your house last week was so volatile, and your condition was so desperate that I left for home drained and dispirited. I beg you to accept the hands held out to you this day. I beg you to take the first step in your healing so that soon, God willing, you will again be my smart, generous, confident sister, the gracious lady I have always been proud to call my sister, my only sister.

Je t'aime, ma couer, ma souer,
Catherine

Paul flies from Portland to Chicago, changes planes, flies to Syracuse, rents a car, and drives to Ithaca. He gets to the hotel shortly before dawn.

Sunday, October 11

I was not there. This is how it was described to me by those who were:

In the morning, the family members meet with the interventionist, Cliff, at the hotel. Then Paul, Ken, Matt, Patrick, Elise, and Cliff caravan to the house in separate cars. They have prepared. They have written impact statements to read that describe their pain. They know to avoid spontaneity, labels, and blame. They have studied the guidelines for interventions, and they agree to adhere to them. They know this is the surest way to convince Pam to confront her illness and consent to treatment.

And they know that at an intervention, anything can happen.

Pam is stunned to see them. As they assemble in her living room, she grows defensive and then, soon, increasingly agitated. Cliff opens the meeting. He has experience in directing interventions. Back in Arizona, his reputation is stellar. Within minutes, though, Pam is beside herself. The orderly progression of an intervention goes out the window. Emotions spiral out of control.

Pam sinks to the floor and wraps her arms around Paul's ankles. Sobbing, speaking in French, she begs her brother to stop the meeting, to make everybody go away, to leave her alone, to let her stay home.

Je t'en supplie! She cries out. I beg you! I'll be good. Please, please, let me stay home! *Laisse-moi rester!*

Paul has had enough. Abruptly, he stands. In the firm tone a parent takes with a disobedient child, he tells his older sister, "Get up, Pam. Go upstairs and pack your clothes. You've got twenty minutes."

Pam instantly quiets. Gathering herself, she rises and turns to the stairs.

They have succeeded. Pam agrees to enter treatment.

The drive from Ithaca to the medical facility should take about three hours. But it doesn't. For some reason, Cliff is driving the lead car, and Cliff doesn't know the way. Pam is in the back seat, between Ken and Matt. Patrick and Elise are following in a second car. Paul closes up the house and leaves Ithaca alone for the long trip back to Oregon.

Cliff tries to navigate unfamiliar roads despite mounting tension in the car. Somewhere between Ithaca and the coastal town where the rehab center is located, Cliff loses his way. Patrick and Elise follow Cliff. Everyone realizes they are lost when they see the Manhattan skyline in the distance. The journey stretches on and on.

Pam's resolve about in-patient treatment is fragile. During the long drive, she begs for breaks. As soon as Cliff slows the car to pull over, she scrabbles over her brother, pushes open the door, drops to the roadside, and curls into a ball of misery. Hours after leaving Ithaca, they arrive at the treatment center.

Cliff and Matt go in first. The news is terrible. A patient scheduled to be released at noon has decided to stay another day. The bed reserved for Pam will not be available until tomorrow.

In a nearby town, they find a hotel with vacancies. They check in, collect the luggage from the cars, and help Pam through the lobby. When the door to the guest room opens, Pam falls apart.

"The windows won't open!" she moans. "I can't do it!"

There is no convincing her.

They troop downstairs, check out, load the luggage into the cars, and drive to another town. By the time they find a hotel with vacancies and with windows that open, it's midnight.

Ken and Matt take turns keeping vigil. Hour after hour, Pam's wretched illness rages, controlling her mind, laying waste to her body, burying her soul. She weeps and paces. Demands and begs. During the night, she soils herself. Her youngest brother cleans her and returns her gently to bed.

Nobody sleeps.

Monday, October 12

The autumn morning sparkles with sunshine. Century-old trees sprinkle the treatment center lawn with colorful leaves. The scene is reminiscent of the grand, old seaside resorts where in the past wealthy New Yorkers and

Bostonians took refuge from the heat, hustle, and tiresome social obligations of the cities.

Matt and Cliff help Pam up the steps and into the lobby. The others wait in the parking area. She falters, twists, tries to return to the car. She heaps blame on everyone, begs to go home, shouts and flails. Two male orderlies take our sister by her elbows and maneuver her through the lobby. At the far end, double doors open by unseen command. The minute the men pilot my raving sister to the other side, the doors close and lock behind her.

"Save me! Save me!"

Her terrified cries echo through the building.

That night, I write to Paul, Ken, Matt, Patrick, and Elise.

> Catherine – Whatever you have accomplished in your life up to now and whatever you accomplish in the future, in a final accounting those things will pale compared with the fact that today you saved a life. That is the hallmark of a hero.

I write to Tom, too. I tell him what happened. He writes back. He says when he read my email, he broke down and cried.

In the coming days, one issue looms large: How long will Pam stay in treatment? I ask her children to trust us to guide the process. I tell them we are firm in our resolve that she stay well past the brief period of detox. I tell them I have asked God to bless their mother.

We assume the hospital staff will convince Pam to complete at least an additional twenty days of psychological evaluation and treatment after the ten-day detox period. Paul offers to work out the financials. He and Matt have each written a personal check to cover Cliff's $5,000 fee. Before Paul left Ithaca, he handed Matt one of his credit cards for the hospital's initial payment. The clerk behind the desk swiped Paul's card for $10,000 as soon as Pam disappeared through the double doors. The card will see another $10,000 hit soon, if Pam stays on.

Paul suggests we focus on Pam getting better and work out the financials later.

About a week later, we are stunned to learn that our sister can walk out of the place after the initial ten-day detox period and another few days of treatment. Paul threatens to fly across the country again and block the door. He says if he has to do that, he's going to be annoyed. He says he's not going to let Pam buffalo her way out of there before she's well.

If the hospital's medical director determines Pam is not an imminent danger to herself or others, if she manages to line up transportation home, and if she has registered for an out-patient treatment program in Ithaca, the medical director will release her. There is nothing Paul or anyone else can do to stop it.

The news leaves us hollowed.

For the better part of a decade, we have dealt with crises and decisions, with responsibilities, disagreements, and sorrows. We did what we could and emerged battered but whole. Now, with an unthinkable tragedy so near, we are powerless. Helplessness deflates our resolve. We live in dread.

Friday, October 16

> Catherine – If she walks out of treatment now, I will place
> primary blame on the hospital. It's their job to convince her to
> stay and to advise her family about any other form of recourse.
> I'll be heartsick. And I'll fully expect the worst.

Paul writes again. He says Pam is afraid of being controlled, and she assumes there is nothing left to live for. He says if she is allowed to leave the hospital, and if she does so, he will cut the cord to her.

> Ken – I can't fathom the depth of misery our sister is
> experiencing, so I am incapable of taking the all-or-nothing
> position on future contact. I feel helpless, too, but I know that is
> a fraction of the helplessness Pam must feel. I will pray.

Matt writes. He says he knows we have all acted out of love and compassion. We have all prayed, and we have reached the end of our rope. He says it's up to Our Lord whether Pam stays on the path to a lasting recovery.

Wednesday, October 21

Pam sends word that she will soon leave the hospital by private limo and go home. She says she has arranged to attend a twenty-eight-day course of out-patient treatment at a facility near Ithaca. She adds that the medical director at the Connecticut hospital supports her decision.

Paul calls Pam. He implores each of us to do the same. It does no good.

Sunday, October 25

Less than two weeks after Pam was brought to the facility, writhing and raving, the staff stands by as she checks herself out.

The Underhills and Pam's children make a pact to check in with her daily, sometimes by phone, sometimes in writing. Soon, Pam's responses fill our email feeds with updates on her steady recovery and happy plans for the future. So bright. So breezy.

So deceptive.

In late November, she tells us she is in the second week of therapy in Ithaca and seeing her doctor once a week. Her energy level is up, and she feels quite a bit better, hasn't had the slightest urge to relapse. She's enjoying the autumn color but looking forward to a first snowfall. She plans to give us all a call before Christmas.

Almost a month ago, right before Pam left the East Coast treatment center, Paul phoned its medical director and read him the riot act. Paul demanded the doctor send the family a signed letter affirming Pam is not a danger to herself or others. As he ended the call, Paul told the director our sister would be dead within thirty days.

Paul was wrong, but not by much.

November afternoons in Ithaca are sunless and sullen. Dusk hovers like fog in lavender-gray verges, waiting, panther-hungry.

I wasn't there. I cannot swear to what happened, precisely when it happened, or even with authority exactly how it happened. But based on first-hand accounts, this is what I think occurred. I would not tell it so if I did not believe it close to the truth.

On Tuesday of Thanksgiving week, Elise and her husband and their children start the two-day car trip to Ithaca, intending to celebrate the holiday with Pam. They arrive Wednesday night, check in at a hotel near her mother's house, and grab a bite at the hotel café.

David, Pam's younger son, arrives at the hotel soon thereafter. He has flown from Christchurch, New Zealand, where he lives and works, for what everyone hopes will be a happy Thanksgiving weekend, a time of renewal, a time to bond again. On the way into town from the airport, David has the taxi driver stop at his mother's house. When no one answers the door, he continues to the hotel, as arranged. He is perplexed but not worried. He thinks his mother is at the store or at the hotel.

She is not. She is inside her house, in the fierce, fulsome grip of madness. In the past days, she has become so shaky and dizzy that she has fallen in her bathroom. More than once. She is cut and bruised and terrified about what would happen if her loved ones see her.

On Wednesday night and again Thursday morning, in a series of emotional phone calls, the plans and preparations for a joyous holiday fall apart. Pam is adamant; she does not want to be seen. Throughout a dolorous Thanksgiving meal at a local restaurant, Elise, her husband, their children, and her brother, David, are barely cognizant of the food, so distraught and disappointed are they. On Friday morning, Elise and her family leave Ithaca for the long drive home. They drop off David at the airport, where he rearranges flights and connections back to New Zealand.

An ill wind sweeps out of the North, dandles the few leaves still clinging to life and limb, and severs their slender moorings. For a magical moment, they dance in the air, a confetti-shower of scarlet and gold. Pam is alone. I doubt she notices; by then, the ephemeral beauty of a leaf-fall is beyond her comprehension.

On Saturday, as planned, Patrick and his wife fly from their home in Kentucky to Ithaca. Unaware of the previous turmoil, they hurry to catch the final two days of the family reunion. At the front door of his childhood home, Patrick sees newspapers littering the stoop, and he frowns. He knocks, waits, rings the bell, knocks harder. He pushes aside a low bush and peers in a window. With growing anxiety, he tries the overhead garage door and a rear service door to the garage. Locked. He sprints to the front door again and rattles the handle. Nothing. Truly worried now, he calls the police.

It's a nice house, not huge or lavish, but nice. Red brick on the bottom, white siding on the second story, black shutters at the windows. A patio out back. Pam tucked her children into their beds in the house, kissed them goodnight hundreds of times, thousands. At the dinette table, she stayed up late to wrap toy trucks and dolls at Christmas. In the kitchen, she baked strawberry rhubarb pies, just as her mother had done at Thornhill. She hung curtains, planted bulbs, ironed her husband's shirts, played piano, studied French, read Proust, transitioned from full-time motherhood to a successful career. All the while, peace of mind eluded her. As her world narrowed, she regarded the house as her only safe zone.

They found her in her house.

In the early 1960s, when the house was built, workers installed a small area of ceramic tile on the floor of the foyer. The idea was to have a spot to deposit muddy or dusty shoes, so they wouldn't leave dark stains on the carpeting. But what if the darkness is inside?

They found her in her safe place.

She had baked a holiday cake. She had ordered yellow and orange mums and arranged them in a vase which she set on the dining room table. Her children, she knew, would notice, and they would conclude she is well.

A squad car pulls into the drive behind Patrick's rental car. The officers force open the service door to the garage. Before they enter the house, one of them lifts the lid of a trash can. Empty bottles fill the bin. The officers tell Patrick to wait in the garage while they enter the house.

They found her inside, near the front door.

The carpeted staircase has a small landing near the bottom. From there, the risers and treads march straight up to the second floor. The flight of stairs hugs the wall on one side and is open on the other side across a spindled banister.

They found her on the foyer floor.

The officers note there are smears of blood on the stairs. I was told the pattern was inconclusive as to whether the stains originated at the bottom or the top, or perhaps went both ways.

Maybe she lost her balance in the upstairs bathroom, hit her head on the sink or the countertop, and, feeling woozy, accidentally tumbled down to the foyer. Maybe she got halfway down and stumbled the rest of the way, opened a wound on her forehead or chin when she struck the ceramic tile floor of the foyer, lost consciousness, and died. Or maybe she made her way back up the stairs to get a bandage, but was so sick, weak, and wounded, that she slid back down.

Maybe, aching for an end to her pain, yearning for death, she threw herself down the stairs on purpose, and when she found herself at the bottom, bloodied but alive, she crawled back up and cast herself down again.

I will never know for sure how my sister died. I do not want to know.

What I know is that the physicality of it must have been brutal. I was told her eyeglasses traveled across the living room.

By the time they found her, we'd already lost her.

At dusk, the temperature falls. Fifty-mile-an-hour winds scour the last brittle petals from my sister's stubbled garden. The newspapers on her porch flutter. Currents of wintry air catch the edges. Pages inked with the news of the day fly away, lost to heartless night.

Catherine and Pam, c. 1951

Chapter 38
Florida
Nov. 30, 2009

Have you heard from Pam?

IT IS 79 DEGREES in Southwest Florida. The skies are sunny, the winds calm at six miles per hour. Golf weather. Take a bike ride and splash in the pool weather.

Dennis and I have bought a condominium in Bonita Springs. Claire, Dan, and Meg have come down for Thanksgiving. Everyone's had a full day. Dennis is fixing cocktails. I'm arranging shrimp on a platter. The next generation has flopped on the living room sofa and is engrossed in a movie.

My cell phone rings. It's Matt. I take the call in a bedroom and close the door.

Matt asks how our vacation is going. He tells me about his holiday dinner in Yuma. We talk about golf for a moment. I am lulled into thinking it's a social call. It isn't.

Finally, I ask, "Have you heard from Pam?"

"Cath," he says, his voice breaking, "she died."

It is unholy, the primal sound that comes from somewhere so deep within me I didn't know it existed. A strange, profoundly disturbing shriek. Raw emotion made audible.

I drop to the floor and throw the phone across the room. What more need I hear?

Dennis rushes in and continues the call, listening to Matt, speaking in low murmurs as he learns what few details my brother can provide.

Someone has turned off the television. The living room is quiet. Beyond the pool, palm fronds rustle and then still. Shore birds move on.

The keening of a devastated sister who broke her promise goes on and on.

Eulogy for My Sister
Mary Pamela Underhill
1946 – 2009

Who calibrates a lifetime?

TIME IS A willful thing. It dawdles like the snail-crawl of eternity and races like the wingbeat of a moth. A week ago, it ticked along steady as a metronome. Earth spun west-to-east, as always, half in light, half in darkness. In Ithaca, New York, the sun breasted the horizon and commenced another low journey across a vaulted November sky.

One blink of an eye. One swing of a pendulum marking time on an unwatched clock. In the time it took my sister to fall out of this world and into the next, the heart of everyone who loved and lost her beat once.

A second, an instant, an hour, a decade. Sixty-three years and five months. But who calibrates a lifetime? Who says this one is too long, that one too brief?

I had a sister once, forever. Just one. In brothers, I am surfeit. In sisters, I am bereft.

When Pam and I were little, we slept in side-by-side beds in a room with deep closets for games of hide and seek, with fairytale wallpaper for sweet dreams and Venetian blinds at windows that angled up and down, admitting the world in even doses. We thought nothing of sharing a hairbrush, a bubble bath, a toothbrush. Everything I wore was something my sister had outgrown. I stepped into saddle shoes that conformed to the planes and knobs of her feet. I shrugged into tartan plaid coats and velvet leggings that retained the innocent scent of her.

My sister was a rare woman. Born to material comfort, she was by instinct generous. Bestowed with pale, incandescent beauty, she was unblemished by vanity, a porcelain-skinned teen who yearned in vain to tan, who waged a lifelong war with her naturally wavy hair, who viewed the world through corrected lenses (would that we all could see the world, corrected.)

My sister was endowed with a maternal disposition and God gave Pam two sons and a daughter. I can almost see her, enveloped in bliss, as one by one she held the swaddled infants she had brought into the breathing world, marveling at a tiny out-poked fist, a milky yawn, a shock of hair. She was a mother who took seriously her role as a motivator. She watched from the bedroom door each night as her children knelt to pray the Our Father. When the ponds of New York froze, she drove her kids to the park and waited in a wood shelter, hot chocolate at the ready, while they traced etchings in the ice, skating smooth as glaziers. She signed them up for music lessons and encouraged after school baseball and football. On Ash Wednesday one year, she announced the family would abstain from television; it was mid-summer before the kids realized Lent was long over. And on one memorable occasion, she ferried Patrick, her older son, to the public library for a sewing class.

My sister was intelligent and diligent, a gifted writer and a voracious reader. At fifty-five, she determined to work her way through the *New York Times* List of One Hundred Greatest Books—works by Flaubert and Chekhov, Plato and Proust, George Eliot, Mark Twain, Shakespeare. It took her two years. She emerged triumphant.

Pam was an astute, self-taught investor who built a successful career. She enjoyed her role as vice president of the company she and her former husband founded.

Ever a lady, Pam stood out a mile in airports, outfitted in a full-skirted dress, heels and hose, perfect hair and makeup, even when the destination was a beach house on Fripp Island.

As a girl, she had a crush on Bobby Darin. Later, she graduated to Italian opera. Once a year or so, she flew from Ithaca to Manhattan, where she splurged on a room at a fine hotel and tickets to the New York Philharmonic. She played a wicked game of tennis. She beat me at Scrabble, the stinker.

Today we grieve her passing, each in our own way. Grief is among the most personal of emotions, whether it endures or dissipates, destroys or empowers, tests long-held beliefs, instills perspective, or kindles compassion.

One week ago today in the pearl-white sky above Ithaca, a morning star shook itself from slumber behind ribbons of cloud. Heaven-sent, it drifted to Earth, to New York, to Ithaca, pausing for the span of a heartbeat above a well-kept house on a well-kept lane, bathing my sister in alabaster light.

Chapter 39
After
2009

So many intentions

AFTER THE WAKE and funeral Mass, after the slow, sickeningly familiar drive to Resurrection Cemetery, after prayers at the grave, after unbearable shock melts into rivers of pain, I stare unseeing at the plastic grass that covers the open grave.

My thoughts wander. Two days ago, I sat in silence in Dr. Donna's office, struggling for words. Finally, she asked, "How is your sister?"

I looked at my hand, knotted in my lap, and barked out, "Dead!"

For once, it was the doctor who gasped and startled, not the patient.

Well, what did my psychiatrist expect? What should any of us have expected, we who left Pam by herself? We who knew full well her life was in peril and abandoned her with nothing but a wish and a prayer that somehow, in an unfathomable way, she would heal.

What did we expect? Tragedy was inevitable.

The day we bury my sister, the weather is raw. We linger awhile at the cemetery, chilled to the bone, and finally return to the cars. Elise has arranged a late afternoon supper at a Clayton restaurant. The staff serves a fine meal we do not taste and hardly notice. Afterward, we hold our coffee cups overlong. The waiters stand back; it is clear we are a shattered family. Finally, we move to the lobby and stand in small clots.

We promise to stay in touch, to call one another often, soon. We'll write, too. For sure. Maybe even plan a family reunion. At Paul's place in the wine country, or at Fripp.

We reminisce a while about Fripp, about filling a beach house almost every summer, collecting seashells and building sandcastles, boiling mounds of shrimp our mother bought at the roadside market a few yards from the boats, and about starlight walks along the beach.

Fripp. Ever since that last disastrous beach vacation when Mother was so ill, I have partitioned the past ten years into episodes. Fripp. Her first grave illness and subsequent decline. The flare-up in Dad's den. New York Fashion Week. The World Trade Center attacks. Post-Traumatic Stress Disorder. A hospice in the desert. *Be a good girl. Be a good boy.* The homeless man. Thornhill, trashed. Caregivers who came and went. LaVerne and Shirley, who stayed. Emails, debates, crises. Wills, directives, lawyers. Brittle bones. A ramp, a chair lift, a bed rail, a wheelchair, a closet filled with oxygen canisters. Spiders, wasps, mold, asbestos. *Silent night, holy night.*

Eulogies for my father, my uncle, my aunt, my mother, my sister.

Graduation ceremonies. Paris with Meg. Italy with Claire. Alaska, England, Ireland, and Cabo with Dennis. Oh my patient, kind, steadfast husband, were it not for you.

Thornhill stands empty for more than a year. One day, heavy equipment rumbles up the drive. Bulldozers bash, smash, claw, and scrape. Within hours, trucks haul away pieces of Bob and Merrilee Underhill's dream home, the house where they reared six children, the house where they grew old together, the house they would not leave.

I phone the new owners and ask if I could have six of the bricks scattered across the property, left behind.

"Sure," the man says. "I have no use for them."

My father did. Working on his knees at night and on weekends, Dad built a brick walkway from the top of the drive to our front door and another around back to the patio that was a favorite summer gathering spot for decades.

I intend to keep one brick and send each of my brothers one. Like so many intentions long on sentiment and short on practicality, I never get to it.

Eventually, the new owners build a 9,310-square-foot mansion on the property. The post-modern house spreads its footprint across once-virgin soil where hunters in breechcloths and moccasins stalked game, and where a young man from the city built a white frame house, put up a barn, and tilled fields, a farm he passed down to his children, and they to theirs. Eventually, the orderly rows of corn, beans, squash, and pumpkins growing on a swell of dark Missouri soil caught the eye of Thornhill's developer. By then, suburban St. Louis was approaching rural Missouri. The subdivision developer knocked on the farmer's door. Not long after, men in business suits came to pace off the fields, careful of their shoes as they jotted notes and numbers with Waterman pens. Soon, the rolling hills and brushy declines were pocked with great, gaping holes. Ranch houses with walk-out basements and two-story colonials with Jeffersonian porticos rose almost overnight. By then, the only vestige of the old hunting grounds was an occasional arrowhead plucked from a creek by kids on their way to a tennis court or deep-water pool, or to no particular place at all in the fenceless universe of yesteryear.

When the pale gray mansion that replaced Thornhill has stood a while, it will show its age, and the land beneath it will be more valuable than the house. Bulldozers will rumble up the drive, and the mansion will vanish to make way for the next new thing.

Not vanish. Not entirely. The Thornhill house and the Chafford Woods house live on in old photographs I have saved, in letters, cards, and emails, and in the soft-focus cinema of memory.

In this way, Thornhill stands to this day, anchored to bedrock in my heart, as are my parents who built the house, my sister and our brothers who ran its halls, the family dogs who assumed they owned the place, and the grandchildren who explored its closets for long-forgotten mementos, searched its creek for arrowheads, and gave themselves over to unencumbered sleep in bedrooms named for little boys and girls who had not been little in a long time.

A house is a building, but a home is something else entirely. More than wood, bricks, and mortar, it is a place of shelter, safety, and camaraderie, a concept as abstract and unique as it is material. A home is the aggregation of many things.

Children dragging blankets and pillows from their beds for games under the eaves. Holiday dinners served on plates rimmed with gold. Papier-mâché animals marching along windowsills. Ice skates hanging by their laces and bicycles teetering on training wheels. Windows with views of a make-believe world where knights gallop on horses with tails of silk. Saturday morning pancakes slathered with syrup and Sunday morning caramel rolls warm from the oven.

Batting practice in the yard. Tadpoles in mayonnaise jars. Tools on pegboard in the garage. Library books on nightstands in the bedrooms. Dog baths in the standing tub.

More. So much more.

Toboggan rides down to the edge of the creek. Ping-Pong tournaments in the basement. An American flag out front. A statue of St. Francis out back. Bird dogs named Patsy. A home perm that failed. Sewing lessons that succeeded. Calculus and tears. Contact lenses and tears. Trophies on shelves. Rosaries in drawers. A chess table by the fireplace. A Model T truck in the garage. Singleton socks in the laundry room.

Well after my father died in a desert hospice, after my mother drowned in a bed, after strangers stole her identity and a vagrant fouled their home, even after bulldozers rumbled up the drive and took the place to ground, I see it still, miss it still.

Thornhill.

Chapter 40
Beams of Gold
May 2015

Snow-capped peaks

IN THE TELLING of these years, I have devoted much of my energies to my newspaper career and to the Underhill family, but any assumption that Dennis, Claire, and Meg are of lesser importance to me is unthinkable.

Dennis is my constant. I am the spark-shower in his July sky. We are as different from one another as can be, which I guess is the beauty of it. Even now, well into our fourth decade of marriage, he waits to sit at the dinner table until I am seated and calls out a cheery goodbye when he walks to the mailbox, courtesies born of respect that time and familiarity have not dimmed.

Educated by Jesuits, Dennis long ago identified the values most worthy of holding dear. Among them was an unwavering commitment to family. He is a man of gentle humor whose kindness and intelligence define him, an indulgent and loving father, a husband so willing to please his wife that I have learned to rein in what I want. Somewhat.

He and I have shared every unremarkable day and every spectacular moment of our adult lives. That's how it was and is and will continue to be because that's how we wish it to be.

Almost three years after Claire and Dan stood on a sun-dappled hilltop and exchanged wedding rings, our first grandchild was born. It took some doing, but after forty hours of labor Lillian Leslie Gould emerged. Mother and baby were fine, although momentarily the worse for their exertions.

I admire the ways Claire and Dan are rearing their daughter, with trial and error, as all parents do, with established boundaries and boundless love, rivers of affection, and occasional exasperation. They research traditional and modern theories, seek guidance from peers on social media, and trust their instincts. Nearly every weekend, they head to the mountains to hike, ski, or camp under the stars with Lillian.

My Claire is wicked funny. She is far more well-read than I will ever be. Like her grandfather, she is a baker of pies. His were Navy-grade. Hers belong on the cover of glossy magazines. Do not ask Claire to hem a skirt, iron a shirt, fold socks into neat rows in a drawer, or answer her phone. She won't. But when it comes to what truly matters—hosting guests in her home, arranging family vacations, and reading bedtime stories to Lillian slowly and expressively, even when Lillian plucks the longest book from the shelf—Claire won't let you down. She is a committed, demonstrative teacher, and her students reward her with affection and progress.

Throughout their lives, my daughters have resembled each other in appearance and differed in temperament. At no time was this more apparent than on their rainy wedding mornings.

In the bridal suite at Wisconsin's Whistling Swan Inn, Claire sequestered in the bathroom and railed at the weather. In the bridal suite at the Stanley Hotel in Estes Park, Colorado, Meg passed the hours chatting with her best friend, her sister, her mother, and her niece. When Lillian plucked the pair of satin bridal slippers from an open shoebox, stuck her feet in them and clomped around the room, Meg smiled indulgently and asked if anyone had a camera.

Meg is most comfortable in a logical and orderly world. She prefers reason to conflict. She manages unknown or unsettled situations with meticulous preparation and an outer calm that belies the effort it takes to appear so. This developed early.

When Meg was a little girl, she would get so excited before a family vacation that she could not sleep for days beforehand. Finally, to avoid having an exhausted, miserable child on the opening end of a trip, Dennis and I and Claire formed a cabal of silence. We filled our suitcases and hid them. We didn't breathe a word in front of Meg. On the morning of our departure, I would tap Meg.

"Wake up, honey. We're leaving for Disney World right after breakfast!"

It was abrupt, and the poor little thing was momentarily bewildered, but it worked.

During medical school and her infectious diseases residency at Northwestern University Medical Center in Chicago, Meg yearned to be in a relationship of committed love.

In the summer of 2013, a friend asked if she'd like to meet someone. "He went to Notre Dame," the friend said. "He lives here in Chicago. He's a lawyer. A patent lawyer."

Meg's first dates with Bryan Leitenberger went well. The relationship took off.

Two years after they met, Meg and Bryan married on the grounds of a historic hotel in the Rocky Mountains. The setting was cinematic: rows of white chairs on a sweep of lawn. A massive, old world hotel beyond a stand of pine trees. Across a valley dotted with shops and restaurants, a mountain range rose to the sky, its smooth peaks bleached by the season's last snow.

Shortly after dawn, clouds boiled overhead. Pelting rain drenched the chairs, matted the grass, and turned the walking paths to mud. The bride, the groom, and the wedding planner conferred in three-way cell phone calls. Reluctantly, they agreed to consider an indoor vow ceremony, but only if hell froze over. Through the day, rain continued to fall. In the late afternoon, wedding guests gathered in the lobby. Some carried umbrellas. Bryan and the wedding planner kept vigil under an outdoor portico, scanning the skies, checking weather apps on their phones, and belaying updates to Meg.

Finally, the clouds parted. Hotel staffers wiped down each white chair. A quartet of musicians began to play, and strains of classical music drifted into air thick with springtime scents. Ninety guests emerged from the lobby and took their seats. The groom walked down the grassy center aisle and turned to face his guests. He cast his gaze well beyond them, though, and scanned the hotel doorways for a glimpse of Meg. In the few interminable moments before she emerged, he tucked a hand in his jacket pocket, removed it, smoothed nonexistent wrinkles, and finally relaxed—somewhat—when his brother rose from the front row and stood at his side.

She was incandescent, my Meg. A willowy bride in an off-the-shoulder gown of imported lace that set off her fair complexion. A bouquet of deep scarlet flowers added a dash of drama. Tucked into her upswept hair was a pearl and diamond brooch, a gift from my mother to me, and now from me to Meg. Dennis presided over the vows. Behind him, massifs rose to majestic heights.

In the waning of the day, in a cathedral of God's making, Meg and Bryan pledged their hearts and lives to one another. In the distance, the sun hovered like a crown over the highest peak. The last of its chiffon beams fanned down the mountainside, bathing the lovers in celestial light.

Today, Meg is an infectious diseases doctor at a university medical center, and Bryan is a patent lawyer with international clients. Their son likes toy trucks and tool kits and bacon, riding on the back of his father's bike, clearing the driveway with the leaf blower, and trains. Most of all, trains. Their baby daughter enjoys chewing on her brother's train tracks only slightly less than nibbling on her toes.

We love them dearly.

From the gut-twisting merger of Milwaukee's newspapers in 1995 to the heart-rending funeral for my sister in 2009, the constancy of my husband's love and the joy my daughters bring to my life are what held the pieces of me together.

At times, it seemed as if every turn of a calendar page gave fresh opportunity to heartache or joy. One moment I was washing dishes in Thornhill's kitchen and within the hour I was fleeing my childhood home in tears. One day I was in Rockefeller Center watching supermodels walk a runway and the next day I was swept into an epic disaster.

They were years of obligation, opportunity, and irony. My father, an East Coast boy, died in Arizona. My mother, who fought to live out her days at Thornhill, was too sick in the end to die in her house. The Underhill siblings, who stood to inherit substantial sums of money, quarreled about everything but money.

From our earliest days, the children of Bob and Merrilee Underhill have been an amalgam of distinct individuals. A willful one. An obsequious one. A funny one, an academic, an athlete or two. A popular one, a dependable one, a waffler. A leader and a follower. A procrastinator and a delegator. But it would be wrong to regard any of us as a hero or a villain. At times, life is messy. Ours sure was. But in the aggregate, we are a single entity, fused to one another because we want to be, and because we work at it.

During more than a decade of crises, the bonds of kinship had every reason to fray, and did. But they did not sever. Every sarcastic accusation and lacerating retort that might have forever separated us, didn't. Every absence that seemed unforgivable and ultimatum cast as final, wasn't. When it seemed as if the fissures that divided us could not be breached, we found a path. Even during the worst periods, we understood that beneath a veneer of distrust, selfless motives drove us.

It might seem as if I staggered from one seismic crisis to the next, but that's not how it was. On most days, nothing of note happened. I wrote newspaper stories, bought groceries, met friends for coffee, took walks, made dinner. In those tranquil periods, my husband, my daughters, and my friends were the tonic that kept despair at bay and helped me restore the hope I had all but lost to PTSD.

Chapter 41
Tribute

September 2021

Long moments in reverie

I STILL HAVE a tough time getting through the month of September. Still startle easily. Still hate to walk under scaffolding and drive under bridges, still have an acquired fear of huge things collapsing. Still worry about my children, their husbands, their children, my husband. But I do not fixate, do not obsess. With personal resolve and professional oversight, I continue to heal what once hurt and mend what was once broken.

Years after I went to college dreaming of a career as a West Wing speechwriter, I finally started writing speeches. I enjoyed giving author talks after my first book was published in 2010. In time, I was asked to speak at USA Today Storyteller events and to give presentations through a program sponsored by Florida Gulf Coast University.

Each September 11th, I stand at a podium and retrace my footsteps in New York. Images of the attacks flash on a screen behind me. As wrenching as it is, I feel called to share an eye-witness account of that tragic event and its aftermath with those who watched it on television or who were born after it took place. And on a personal level, the talks I give validate my work as a journalist that defining week.

Over the years, the *Milwaukee Journal Sentinel* has observed important anniversaries of 9/11 by publishing a lengthy article and posting a video that reprise its staffers' coverage of the attacks. But on each solemn anniversary, the account it disseminates is incomplete, for it makes no mention of my award-winning reporting that week. In redacting the contributions of the only *Milwaukee Journal Sentinel* reporter to file eyewitness bulletins from New York on 9/11, the *Journal Sentinel* has recast the record of its own history.

In September of 2021, on the twentieth anniversary of the attacks, I stood again at a podium as images of the World Trade Center flickered across a screen behind me. The audience that filled rows of chairs included a former combat veteran, a woman who had cared for her father during his last illness, and a toddler. The child was quiet, content to sit enfolded in her mother's arms. It was a portrait of bliss that transported me to moments of profound contentment in my past.

After Claire and then Meg brought each of their newborn babies home from the hospital, I stayed on a week or so to assemble casseroles, launder cradle sheets, and shop for groceries while the new moms and dads bonded with their infants. Sometimes, I took one of the night bottle feedings. Afterward, I would stand at a window bathed in moonbeams and sing "Oh Shenandoah" to the milk-fed wonder in my arms, sing softly and slowly to the part about crossing the wide Missouri River, and then start at the beginning again.

Attendant upon every gurgle and murmur, oblivious to the machinations of the outer world, the city lights, the distant traffic, I would pass long moments in reverie, swaying in the way grandmothers and mothers holding babies ever have swayed, gliding side-to-side shifts that have lulled infants born centuries apart, infants separated by oceans and continents, by malleable borders and immutable mountains, newborns who come to us in all colors, who will differ in creed, language, and lore, and who will live in circumstances from dismal poverty to glittering luxury. Each mewling child arrives intrinsically unique, and yet within his or her every cell and molecule are traces of those who came before—the gray blue of a mother's eyes, the agility of an athletic father, the sparkling laugh of a great-grandmother, the swirl of a cowlick, an aptitude for carpentry, music, numbers, letters, golf. Inscribed on the helixes of the children we bring squalling into the world is a vast unwritten library of stories, generations of family deeds recorded in every iteration and elaboration of sorrow and joy that course the human heart, and that sculpt the dazzling, distant realms of the soul.

"The post is just going, which forces me in great haste to conclude."[16]
— Jonathan Swift

Note

For most of my life, I was unacquainted with the reality of Post-Traumatic Stress Disorder. When put to the question, I would have said it was a modern term for the "shell shock" that afflicted some soldiers who came back from combat duty. But that is a deceptively narrow definition.

In general terms, PTSD is a condition some people develop after they see or are in some way involved in a traumatic event—a violent assault or fatal car accident, a fire or flood. A school shooting or terrorist act.

The American Psychiatric Association defines PTSD as a condition in which a person exposed to a traumatic event experiences for more than one month symptoms unattributable to other conditions. A partial list of PTSD symptoms includes:

a) Intrusion – Memories, flashbacks, or sensations connected to the trauma which the person can't control.

b) Avoidance – Blocking anything, including memories, which remind him/her of the event.

c) Two alternations in thought or mood – For example, anxiety, depression, guilt, lack of emotion, lack of engagement.

d) Two changes in arousal or reactivity – Such as angry or reckless behavior, difficulty sleeping and/or concentrating.

In the spring of 2001, I joined the ranks of journalists who live with a range of PTSD symptoms.

Unbeknown to me, clinical studies and academic research were underway even before the World Trade Center disaster. Eventually, the findings would show that a majority of journalists have been exposed to one or more work-related traumatic events, situations that place them at risk for long-term PTSD.

According to the research, risk factors to journalists for developing PTSD include exposure to highly intense assignments, traumatic events in one's personal life, a prior history of depression, competition with colleagues, and feelings of guilt about the traumatic event.

According to the findings of a study posted on the website of Columbia University's Dart Center for Journalism & Trauma, more organizational (newsroom) support for staffers exposed to trauma could reduce mental health harm and lead to increased job performance.[17]

The end of my journalism career is a separate issue in this memoir. Below is a bit of context:

In May of 2003, the career of *New York Times* reporter Jason Blair veered off path after editors at the *Times* discovered he had plagiarized the work of others, among other serious transgressions.[18]

Newspapers across the country began examining the work of some of their staffers and reprimanding and dismissing those whose work did not stand up to scrutiny. Four years later, a doctoral dissertation based on known cases of plagiarism at U.S. daily newspapers concluded that the number of exposed incidents roughly tripled in the wake of the Jason Blair fiasco, and that the number of cases resulting in dismissal increased after Blair, as well.[19]

Credits

[1] River Smith, Elana Newman, Susan Drevo, Autumn Slaughter, *Covering Trauma: Impact on Journalists*, July 1, 2015. Article posted on the Dart Center for Journalism & Trauma web site providing an overview of research on occupational hazards for journalists covering traumatic events and risk factors. Originally published by River Smith and Elana Newman, January, 2009; Updated by Susan Drevo, May, 2016, and Autumn Slaughter, March, 2019. https://dartcenter.org/content/covering-trauma-impact-on-journalists

[2] Jonathan Swift, "A Tale of a Tub," *The Works of the Rev. Jonathan Swift*, Vol. 2, Sec. V, 1710.

[3] Catherine Fitzpatrick, *Daily Mindfulness: 365 Days of Present Calm, Exquisite Living*, Familius LLC, 2020 https://www.familius.com/familius-authors-share-what-fatherhood-means-to-them

[4] Catherine U. Fitzpatrick, *Voyage, A Memoir of Love, War, and Ever After*, eLectio Publishing, 2017.

[5] Catherine Fitzpatrick, "Birds of Paradise," Outrider Press Black and White Anthology, Sept. 2010.

[6] War reporters, Military History Matters, Jan. 20, 2020, https://www.military-history.org/feature/modern-articles/war-reporters-kate-webb.html.

[7] Amy Tikkanen, *Timeline of the September 11 Attacks*, https://www.britannica.com/list/timeline-of-the-september-11-attacks.

[8] Catherine Fitzpatrick, "Sounds and Fury," https://www.halfwaydownthestairs.net, Sept. 2010.

[9] Catherine Fitzpatrick, "On the Way to Heaven," Write City Magazine, Chicago Writers Association, March 15, 2015.

[10] Bebeto Matthews, "The stories of Sept. 11 lie beneath Brooklyn", Associated Press, Sept. 11, 2006.

[11] Catherine U. Fitzpatrick, *Voyage, A Memoir of Love, War, and Ever After*, eLectio Publishing, 2017.

[12] Catherine Fitzpatrick, Daily Mindfulness: 365 Days of Present Calm, Exquisite Living, Familius LLC, 2020 https://www.familius.com/familius-authors-share-what-fatherhood-means-to-them

[13] Catherine Fitzpatrick, "How Teenie is the Bikini," *Milwaukee Journal Sentinel*, June 6, 2003.

[14] Peter Robertson, "The Bikini Bungle," *Milwaukee Magazine*, October 2003.

[15] Peter Robertson, "The Greater of Two Evils," *Milwaukee Magazine*, November 2003.

[16] The Rev. Jonathan Swift, "A Discourse Concerning the Mechanical Operation of the Spirit," *The Works of The Rev. Jonathan Swift*, Vol. 2, 1710.

[17] River Smith, Elana Newman, Susan Drevo, Autumn Slaughter, *Covering Trauma: Impact on Journalists*, July 1, 2015, https://dartcenter.org/content/covering-trauma-impact-on-journalists

[18] Dan Barry, David Barstow, Jonathan D. Glater, Adam Liptak, Jacques Steinberg, research support by Alain Delaquérière and Merrilee Wilder, "Correcting the Record," *New York Times*, May 11, 2003.

[19] Norman P. Lewis, *Paradigm Disguise: Systemic Influences on Newspaper Plagiarism*, PhD diss., Philip Merrill College of Journalism, 2007.

PTSD Risk Factors and Symptoms Affecting Journalists

Research and scholarly studies published since 2001 have examined work-related exposures and mental health issues among journalists. https://pubmed.ncbi.nlm.nih.gov/28834207/ Among the findings, conclusions, and suggestions are:

1. Mental health issues are a more serious concern in journalism than among other professions.

2. Journalists are particularly vulnerable due to exposure to work-related tragic and traumatic events on a regular basis. These events include acts of violence, accidents, natural disasters, deaths, conflicts and wars, death penalty executions, random shootings, terrorist bombings, sexual assaults, domestic violence, and suicides. (Dworznik, 2011; Feinstein et al., 2014; Feinstein et al, 2002; Newman et al., 2003; Pyevich et al., 2003; Simpson & Boggs, 1998; Smith et al., 2017; Teegen & Grotwinkel, 2001; Dworznik, 2011; Feinstein et al, 2002; Newman et al., 2003; Pyevich et al., 2003; Smith et al., 2017; Teegen & Grotwinkel, 2001.)

3. Factors that can negatively affect the mental health of journalists include chasing deadlines, perfecting the craft of producing content, constant competition with other media organizations, dealing with horrifying graphic or pictorial elements, lack of job security, longer or irregular working hours, and less time for family interaction and socialization.

4. Journalists suffer from a variety of psychological disorders, including depression, anxiety, obsessive-compulsive disorder, post-traumatic disorder (PSTD), drug or alcohol addiction, insomnia, food disorder, high professional burn out, feelings of guilt, failure to handle daily pressures.

5. Training and work culture foster a belief that journalists are immune to the impact of violence and tragedy and resilient to whatever they face in their professional life, but efforts to remain distant from the issues and events they cover sometimes lead journalists to feel guilt.

Mental Health Risk Factors for Journalists

1. Exposure to high intensity assignments/traumatic assignments, Backholm & Björkqvist, 2010; Dworznik, 2011; Feinstein et al., 2002; Pyevich et al., 2003; Smith et al, 2017.

2. Exposure to traumatic events in one's personal life
 Backholm & Björkqvist, 2010; Newman et al., 2003; Smith et al., 2017; Frauke Teegen & Maike Grotwinkel, 2001.

4. Prior history of depression
 Backholm & Björkqvist, 2012.

5. Competition with colleagues
 Monterio et al., 2015.

6. Feelings of guilt about the traumatic event
 Browne et al., 2012.

Published Articles on Trauma and Journalism

Covering Trauma: Impact on Journalists
An overview of current research on the occupational hazards for journalists covering traumatic events, risk factors that aggravate those effects, and suggestions for mitigating those factors. River Smith, Elana Newman, Susan Drevo, Autumn Slaughter, July 1, 2015.
Originally published by River Smith and Elana Newman in January, 2009; Updated by Susan Drevo in May, 2016, and by Autumn Slaughter in March, 2019.
 https://dartcenter.org/content/covering-trauma-impact-on-journalists

Trauma-related guilt and post-traumatic stress among journalists.
An article describing the results of a 2012 study that explored the psychological impact of exposure to work-related trauma among journalists. Tess Browne, Michael Evangeli, Neil Greenberg.
https://pubmed.ncbi.nlm.nih.gov/22522737/

Journalists' emotional reactions and psychological distress after working with a school shooting.
An article based on 2012 research study. Klas Backholm, Kaj Björkqvist. First published August 21, 2012.
 https://doi.org/10.1177/1750635212440914

A Brief List of Online Resources
(Digital addresses as of December 2021)

Dart Center for Journalism & Trauma
https://dartcenter.org
A project of the Columbia University Graduate School of Journalism, the DART Center draws on a global network of news professionals, mental health experts, educators and researchers to provide journalists around the world with the resources to achieve informed, innovative, and ethical news reporting on violence, conflict and tragedy.

National Center for PTSD
https:// www.ptsd.va.gov
Part of the U.S. Department of Veterans Affairs (VA), the center offers information about symptoms, therapies, medications, local care options, assessment tools, and support for family and friends. It maintains an online and phone hotline for US veterans who need help right away.

National Institute of Mental Health
https://www.nimh.nih.gov
NIMH is one of the institutes and centers that make up the National Institutes of Health. Its mission is to advance understanding and treatment of mental illnesses through basic and clinic research. The site provides online links to brochures, fact sheets, statistics, and information about how to get immediate help in a crisis.

American Psychological Association
https://www.apa.org/topics/covid-19/journalists-first-responders

WebMD
https://www.webmd.com/depression/depression-ptsd-vs-depression
An online resource that outlines and clarifies the symptoms of depression and PTSD.

National Suicide Prevention Lifeline
https://suicidepreventionlifeline.org
A network of more than 160 crisis centers providing a 24-hour toll-free phone number available to anyone in suicidal crisis or emotional distress. Call 1-800-273-8255.

Elder care Locator

https://elder care.acl.gov/public/resources/federal_websites.aspx

A public service of the U.S. Administration on Aging that connects families with services for older adults, including a comprehensive list of federal web sites for those seeking information and assistance on Alzheimer's Disease, managing someone else's money, elder justice, government benefits, Medicare, nutrition, Social Security, and travel.

American Association of Retired Persons

www.aarp.org

Provides information and discounts to members for a variety of products and services, from estate planning to wireless telephone plans, from car rental deals to yoga instruction booklets and online flower delivery companies.

Agency for Healthcare Research and Quality

https://effectivehealthcare.ahrq.gov/products/ptsd-adults-trauma-interventions/research-protocol

This agency, part of the U.S. Department of Health and Human Services, provides information about interventions for the prevention of PTSD in adults after exposure to psychological trauma.

Acknowledgements

For their support during the writing of this memoir, I would like to thank:

My husband, Dennis, who lived through it all in real-time, and then again during the years it took me to turn a hot mess of a first draft into a completed memoir.

My daughters, Claire Fitzpatrick Gould and Meg Fitzpatrick, who also lived through it all in real-time.

My sons-in-law, Dan Gould and Bryan Leitenberger, and my grandchildren, Lillian, Nolan, and Maeve, who fill my life with joy.

Kenneth James Underhill, who shares most of my DNA code and many of the experiences in this story, and who has completed his second book, a memoir of his boyhood years at Thornhill.

Michele Derus, a stellar reporter and loyal friend who was at my side during the trials and triumphs of our Milwaukee newspaper years, and who offered thoughtful insights, sent me probing questions, made me delve deeper, and softened each blow with encouragement.

My longtime friend Mary Ann Dowd Sussman, who shored me up when I was drowning, called my attention to missing commas and misplaced modifiers, and occasionally sent me nostalgic photos of mid-century St. Louis, which I liked.

My friends Anne, Shellie, Martha, Marilyn, Kathleen, Deb, Anna Marie, Colleen, and Sandy. What would I do without you?

Elizabeth Engel, former senior archivist at the State Historical Society of Missouri, who accessioned my notebooks and memorabilia from 9/11 into the Society's collections, acknowledging and preserving a record of my contributions to the *Milwaukee Journal Sentinel's* coverage of that world-changing event.

For graciously providing endorsements for *Recorder of Deeds*, I am grateful beyond measure to George Faller, Kathleen Arenz, Anita Lamont, Karen K. Marshall, Carol Cole, Karla Linn Merrifield, Lowell Gerson, Miles Goodwin, Debra Valentina, Damien Jaques, Richard Wood, and my dear brother Kenneth.

Last but certainly not least, a heartfelt thank you to the women of Bedazzled Ink, publishers of *Recorder of Deeds*, whose belief in the power of my story was immediate and whose faith in me is a heartwarming thing, indeed.

Cruise, 2020

Catherine Underhill Fitzpatrick grew up in a large St. Louis family. After graduating from the University of Missouri School of Journalism, she went on to feature writing positions at daily newspapers in Hannibal, St. Louis, and Milwaukee.

On Sept. 11, 2001, Catherine was in Manhattan to cover New York Fashion Week for Wisconsin's largest newspaper. At first word of the terrorist attacks, she rushed to Ground Zero and filed award-winning eyewitness reports. Her notebooks and other mementos from her harrowing experiences that week have been accessioned into the State Historical Society of Missouri archives.

Catherine's articles, stories, and essays have appeared in newspapers, literary reviews, magazines, and anthologies. She is the author of three published books prior to *Recorder of Deeds*.

A seasoned public speaker, Catherine has given author talks and lectures across the Midwest and Southeast. She has been a featured speaker at two USA Today Storytellers Project programs. She is an award-winning member of the Florida Writers Association and a published member and featured speaker of the Chicago Writers Association.

Catherine and her husband, Dennis, live in Denver, Colorado. They have two daughters.

To contact Catherine or schedule an author talk, kindly log on to www.cufitzpatrick.com.

Just aim your phone's camera at the QR Code

www.ingramcontent.com/pod-product-compliance
Lightning Source LLC
Chambersburg PA
CBHW031158270326
41931CB00006B/326